RIDING THE WAVES

An Insider's Memoire

JOURNEY OF A NAVAL ARTIFICER ENGINEER

One Among Thousands Stories

Dinesh Joshi

Chennai • Bangalore

CLEVER FOX PUBLISHING
Chennai, India

Published by CLEVER FOX PUBLISHING 2024
Copyright © Dinesh Joshi 2024

All Rights Reserved.
ISBN: 978-93-56488-21-2

This book has been published with all reasonable efforts taken to make the material error-free after the consent of the author. No part of this book shall be used, reproduced in any manner whatsoever without written permission from the author, except in the case of brief quotations embodied in critical articles and reviews.

The Author of this book is solely responsible and liable for its content including but not limited to the views, representations, descriptions, statements, information, opinions and references ["Content"]. The Content of this book shall not constitute or be construed or deemed to reflect the opinion or expression of the Publisher or Editor. Neither the Publisher nor Editor endorse or approve the Content of this book or guarantee the reliability, accuracy or completeness of the Content published herein and do not make any representations or warranties of any kind, express or implied, including but not limited to the implied warranties of merchantability, fitness for a particular purpose. The Publisher and Editor shall not be liable whatsoever for any errors, omissions, whether such errors or omissions result from negligence, accident, or any other cause or claims for loss or damages of any kind, including without limitation, indirect or consequential loss or damage arising out of use, inability to use, or about the reliability, accuracy or sufficiency of the information contained in this book.

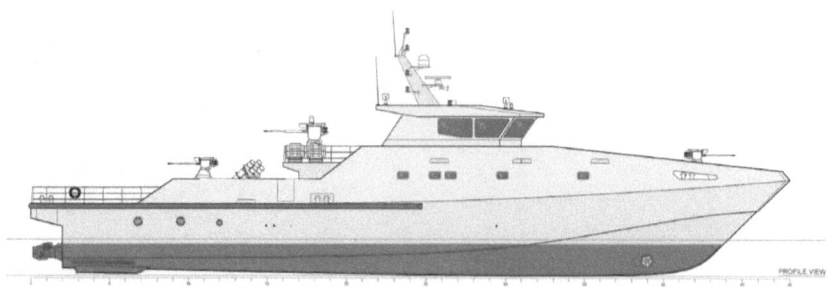

Riding the Waves

PREFACE

This is the story of a journey—a journey spanning over 42 years of resilience, and passion for the maritime industry. As you delve into the pages of this book, you will embark on a voyage through the personal life of a naval engineer, navigating the waters of the Indian Navy, Indian Coast Guard, Corporate, and beyond.

While the events depicted in this book are based on real experiences, the names of the characters have been altered to respect their privacy. Yet, the stories remain as authentic and inspiring as ever.

As the reader delves into the narrative, they will find immersed in the world, where the sea and its vessels become characters. The author, had tried to bring to life the challenges and triumphs of a career dedicated to maritime excellence, drawing upon his profound understanding of the subject matter to paint a vivid and authentic portrait.

In "Riding the Waves," author had weaved together the tapestry of protagonist's life purely from his angle and experience, offering readers a glimpse into the challenges, triumphs, and moments of reflection that shaped his journey. With a profound understanding of the subject matter and a keen eye for detail, author had tried to bring each scene to life, immersing readers in the world of naval engineering and maritime operations.

Preface

The depiction in the book is no way limiting, as same event or action from fellow engineer, crew and colleague's perspective may vary based on their position of strength and understanding. At any point If narration in the book have inadvertently hurt anyone's feeling, author humbly apologises for this mistake.

Throughout these pages, you will witness the protagonist's evolution—from a young, eager recruit to a seasoned professional, navigating the complexities of ship construction, maintenance, and project management. You will share in his triumphs and setbacks, his moments of doubt and determination, and ultimately, his unwavering commitment to his craft.

I invite you to join in this journey, as we navigate the highs and lows of life at sea, and discover the profound meaning of service, dedication, and camaraderie. Through the eyes of our protagonist, may you find inspiration, insight, and a newfound appreciation for the vital work of naval engineers everywhere.

CONTENTS

Preface iv
CONTENTS vi

Part 1. Naval Training 1
   Delhi to Lonavala: A Journey of Aspiration 1
   Trial by Sea: The Selection Process.................................. 3
   Into the Crucible: A Naval Trainee's Journey 6
   Unity in Diversity: Challenges of Journey....................... 9
   Trainees Life- An Eventful Day...................................... 10
   An Endurance Test- Pressure Retention 12
   An Unexpected Shot- Short Lived Freedom................ 13
   Bridging the Gap: Bonds Forged in Naval Engineering 15
   Forging Excellence: The Workshop Chronicles 16
   Balancing Steel and Dreams: Yearning for Youth 18
   Echoes of Rebellion: An Unexpected Night at Training Institute 20
   Collective Solidarity and Camaraderie.......................... 21
   The Wide Arena of Sports 24
   Glimpse of Glamour and Charm................................... 25
   Tides of Change: A Bittersweet Farewell...................... 26
   Navigating Waves and Wonders: A Shipwright's Tale in Bombay... 28

Fun and Play in the Street of Bombay 31
An Altercation- Questioning of Authority 34
Home Away from Home 35
Sports- A Breather from Training 36
Navigating Waves of Change: The Relocation to Vizag 38
Wired for Success: The Naval Electrical Artificer's Journey 40
Skyward Bound: The Wings of Naval Artificer 42
End of an Exciting Journey 44

Part 2. Naval Journey 46

Harmony of Steel and Sea 46
An Electrical Engineer's Odessey 48
A Move- Change of Base Port 49
It's Not all Work- But Sports Too 51
Harbor of Challenges: The Naval Engineer's Odyssey 53
Lord Varuna and Chants of Har-Har Mahadev 55
Mission – Beaching on the Shore 57
Life on a Newly Commissioned Ship 60
Seafarer's Ingenuity: Riding the Waves 62
Life at Sea- A Stormy Affair 64
Flying Machine-Trapped in a Cage 65
A Dreadful Night 67
Seafarer's Symphony: Tale of Repair and Resilience 70
An Artificer's Camaraderie 71
Just into the Marriage- A Sad Parting 74

Exploring The World: A Diplomatic Mission 76
- On International Voyage: A Dream Odyssey 76
- Beginning of an Unforgettable Voyage-Djibouti 76
- Arrival at Port Suez 78
- Bridging Histories: INS Godavari in Sevastopol 80

Contents

- Arrival at Port City Algiers, Algeria..81
- Ponta Del Gada, Azores, Portugal..82
- Sailing the Liberty Seas: Historic US Voyage.............................84
- Country of Great Revolution- Havana, Cuba 86
- Caribbean Call - Sound of Reggae at Kingston, Jamaica..........88
- Steel Drum Rhythm - Port of Spain, Trinidad & Tobago........89
- Garden city of the Caribbean - Georgetown, Guyana..............91
- A 16th Century City - Recife, Brazil..92
- A Picturesque Coastal City- Accra, Ghana.................................94
- Across Gulf of Guinea - Lagos, Nigeria.......................................96
- A Port City with Seafront Promenade - Luanda, Angola 97
- A Sea Voyage from Angola to Mozambique 98
- Life at Maputo, Mozambique 99
- Seychelles, an Indian Ocean Archipelago................................101

Journey Back Home, Bombay 107
Navigating the Depths: A Naval Architect's Odyssey 108
Life in the Home City 110
Turbulence in the Family- Transfer Move 113
A New Beginning - Alas Heavenly 114
Surprise Gurgaon Connection..117
An Island made of Steel- Floating Dry Dock 117
Island Odyssey: A Naval Engineer's Voyage 120
Operation Docking- A Masterpiece of Coordination 120
An Action-packed Workstation- Dock Floor 123
INS Yamuna-A Challenging Task 125
The Unfortunate Docking- Mishap in the Making 126
A Slight Negligence- Mishap in the Waiting 129
Goodbye to The Paradise...130
Waves of Reflection- The Final Voyage 131

Part 3. About Naval Artificer 133
Beyond the Waves: Charting of New Horizons 133
A Bond of Cherished Perseverance 135
EXAM: Sailing Through Generations... 137

Part 4. Maritime Consulting & Documentary Films 140
Sailing Through Frames: Journey into Filmmaking................... 140
Seas of Wisdom- A New Horizon 142
End of an Emerging Idea.. 144
An Unforeseen Voyage: Call to Public Service 145

Part 5. The Coast Guard Journey.. 147
Sailing the Seas of Excellence: A Mentorship 147
Navigating Waters of Excellence: Odyssey in Ship Acquisition... 149
An Inquisitive International Collaboration 151
Navigating the Seas of Innovation: Ship Equipment................. 153
Seas of Success: Role in Coast Guard Ship Construction 154
Ship's Hull Protection- Paint Technology 155
State of Art High Speed Boats -A Challenge.............................. 157
Offshore Patrol Vessel - Acquisition of Excellence 160
Evaluating Right Shipyard -Project OPV.................................... 162
Key Result Area - Vishal's Legacy.. 165
Blessing in Disguise- A God Send Opportunity 166
Final Call- A Change of Track 168

Part 6. ABC Shipyard Journey... 169
Odyssey of Corporate Voyage... 169
In the Heartland of Shipyard... 170
Fury of Monsoon Rain 173
Interceptor Boats-Another Project in Lap.................................. 174

Contents

The Flood Fury- A Force Majeure 175
The Menace of Flood: Casualty Electrical Cables 177
Casualty of the Flood- Interceptor Boats 179
An Australian Connection- Interceptor Boats 180
Innovation in Propulsion Technology- Coast Guard Ships 183
Intricacies of Aluminium Hull Design and Construction 184
Payal's Symphony: A Melody of Sacrifice and Unconditional
Love 186
War of Nerves - A Collateral Damage 188
Building of Defence ship- Plethora of Challenges 191
Symphony of Skill: Construction of the Oil Spill Response
Vessel 192
Ship's Stabilisation - Slow Manoeuvring 195
Harmony of Seas: Symphony of Project Management 196
Safety of Life at Sea and Distress Communication:
IMO Regulations 198
The Aviation Story- Flying Deck Operation 200
Final Test- Inclining Experiment 203
Sailing to Success: Sea Trials of Oil Spill Response Vessel 204
Review Meeting: Grilling Sessions by Government 210
Naval Project - A Merger of Convenience 213
Lost Ship - Revival of the Project 214
An Unusual Reunion- Across the Meeting Table 217
Delivery of Ship -Worth Celebrating 219
Navigating the Storm: Battle Against Financial Turmoil 221

Part 7. Eastern Coast Calling 225
Setting Sail Again: Quest for Professional Fulfilments 225
The Life in City of Joy - Kolkata 227

The Challenges of Work 228
Waves of Reflection: Journey to Rediscovery 229

Part 8. An Entrepreneur Call **232**
An Entrepreneur Journey 232
Life Ahead- A New Beginning 234

About Author *236*

PART 1

NAVAL TRAINING

Delhi to Lonavala: A Journey of Aspiration

At the crack of dawn, amidst missed hustle and bustle of Delhi's crowded streets, on a cold winter morning of Jan 1978, little short of seventeen-years, Vishal stood on the platform of Delhi railway station, his heart pounding with excitement and nervous anticipation. Dressed in his crisply ironed clothes and clutching a suitcase and a handbag containing his belongings, he was about to embark on the journey of a lifetime - leaving behind the familiar comforts of home to pursue his dreams at a naval engineering institute in Lonavala.

As the Frontier Mail train pulled into the station with a deafening roar, Vishal's pulse quickened with anticipation. This would be his first time traveling alone, his first taste of independence and adventure beyond the confines of his hometown. With a deep breath, he boarded the train, his eyes shining with a mixture of excitement and trepidation. As the train chucked, he saw tears rolling down his mother's eyes while his father, with folded hand requested an elderly co passenger to look after him during the journey.

On arrival at Dadar station next morning, he was lost. In the crowd, he stopped a passerby and inquired about the train for Lonavala.

Little later he boarded another train for his destination. The train ride to Lonavala was a whirlwind of sights and sounds, as Vishal watched the landscape change from the bustling streets of Delhi to the serene countryside of Maharashtra. The rhythmic clack of the train on the tracks lulled him into a sense of calm, easing his nerves as he contemplated the journey ahead.

As the train chugged closer to its destination, Vishal's excitement reached a fever pitch. Lonavala, with its lush green hills and crisp mountain air, held the promise of new beginnings and endless possibilities. He could hardly wait to begin his training at the naval engineering institute, to immerse himself in the world of ships and technology, and to forge friendships that would last a lifetime.

Finally, after what seemed like an eternity, the train pulled into the station at Lonavala. With a surge of adrenaline, Vishal stepped onto the platform, his eyes scanning the crowd for any sign of his other candidates like him or any official from training base. And there, amidst the throng of people, he spotted - a group of other young candidates, their faces lit up with smiles of welcome.

As Vishal joined his fellow candidates, he felt a sense of belonging wash over him. Here, among these like-minded individuals, he knew he had found his place in the world. A bus was parked outside station for all those young boys coming from different part of country for their final selection, to proceed to INS Shivaji, a naval training institute for marine engineering. With renewed confidence and determination, he set off towards the institute, ready to embark on the next chapter of his journey. As he walked through the gates of the institute, with its imposing building and sprawling parade ground in front flying Naval Ensign on the pole post, Vishal felt a surge of excitement course through his veins. This was where his dreams would take flight, where he would learn and grow and become the man he was meant to be.

And as Vishal looked back at his first train journey from Delhi to Lonavala, he realized that it was more than just a physical distance covered; it was a symbolic bridge that connected the familiar past with the promising future, setting the stage for a life dedicated to naval engineering and the boundless possibilities that lay ahead- the beginning of a life filled with purpose, passion, and endless possibilities.

Trial by Sea: The Selection Process

As the morning sun cast its golden rays over the Naval Engineering Institute, a group of eager young candidates all gathered in a hall, their hearts pounding with anticipation. Among them was also Vishal, his eyes alight with determination as he awaited the final selection process that would determine his fate.

Vishal, having been an Army NCC cadet for three long years during school days and later Airforce NCC while in first year at college before embarking on his Naval mission, gave him a sense of confidence to pass through, nevertheless he was determined to give his best and not let the guard loose.

The candidates were all ushered into a grand auditorium, where rows of desks awaited them. On each desk lay a stack of papers and a pencil, signalling the written portion of the selection process. Vishal took his seat, his mind buzzing with nervous energy as he prepared to tackle the barrage of questions that lay ahead.

The written test was gruelling, covering a wide range of subjects from science, mathematics to general knowledge. Vishal poured over each question with meticulous precision, drawing upon the knowledge he had acquired in preparation for this moment. As the minutes ticked by, he felt a sense of satisfaction knowing that he had given it his all.

With the written portion complete, the candidates were led to smaller rooms batch by batch, where a panel of psychologists awaited them. This was the psychological evaluation - a crucial step in determining their suitability for the rigorous training that lay ahead. Vishal took a deep breath, steeling himself for whatever challenges awaited him.

The psychologists posed a series of thought-provoking questions, probing into Vishal's motivations, strengths, and weaknesses. They delved into his past experiences, his aspirations for the future, and his ability to handle stress and adversity. Vishal answered each question honestly, drawing upon his inner resolve and determination to succeed. His interactions with fellow candidates were scrutinized, revealing teamwork skills and leadership potential. The psychologists observed every solved puzzle, gesture, every choice, seeking to unearth the qualities that would define a successful naval engineer and officer.

As the evaluation drew to a close, Vishal felt a sense of relief wash over him. He had laid bare his soul before the panel, confident in his ability to meet whatever challenges lay ahead. Now, all that remained was to await the final verdict. Next day was a whirlwind of activities. The morning sun finds all candidates on the sports grounds, sweat glistening on their brows as they push their bodies to the limit. From gruelling obstacle courses to intense endurance drills, they are put through their paces by the stern instructors.

All candidates in a batch of twenty, undergo medical examinations in MI room next day. Some joke and smile seeing other undress in front. Each one wondering why they were asked to bend and cough inside the physical examination room while grinning with laugh. One by one each is taken from one room to other and examined for basic medical checks and parameters recorded. But beneath the surface lies an undercurrent of nervous energy as they wait for outcome.

Days passed; each one filled with anxious anticipation awaited the results of the selection process. Finally, the moment of truth arrived - a list of names pasted on the institute's bulletin board, signalling those who had been chosen to embark on the long journey of training. With trembling hands, Vishal scanned the list until his eyes fell upon his own name. A surge of elation washed over him as he realized that he had been selected, chosen to join the ranks of the Naval Engineering Institute. It was a moment of triumph, a validation of his hard work, dedication, and unwavering determination.

Once emerged selected from rigorous process at INS Shivaji, the list carried the names of hundred successful trainees made through among two hundred fifty called for the final selection. It contained the name of Seventy trainees who would move to Electrical training Institute at Jamnagar, Gujarat.

The batch of seventy aspiring electrical artificer engineers prepared to leave to begin their four-year Naval Artificer Electrical training at INS Valsura in Jamnagar. They all embarked by train on a transformative journey in mid of Jan 1978. Among them was also Ashok, a fellow trainee from Delhi as Vishal, a young man with a passion for all things electrical, ready to immerse himself in the world of naval technology.

Vishal among the thirty, had found mechanical engineering marked against his name in the list, realised that Lonavala is going to be his home for next four years now. As Vishal glanced around the institute once more, he knew that the real journey was only just beginning. But with the strength of his convictions and the support of his fellow candidates by his side, he was ready to face whatever challenges the future might hold. And so, with head held high and heart filled with hope, Vishal embarked on the adventure of a lifetime - a naval journey into the unknown.

Qualified thirty trainees later assembled in the hall post lunch for their briefing. Training commander with his team of instructors, addressed them in a firm and harsh tone and explained about what lies ahead for them in their journey of four years. They would be initially staying together for next six months in Pratapgarh division. Thereafter, all will be distributed among other five divisions housing mixed batches of senior artificer trainees. One of the deputies explained about mess culture, dress codes and do and don'ts when they are in the campus. A tall gentleman from Kerala was introduced as training Instructor, who would brief more about the training next morning.

Into the Crucible: A Naval Trainee's Journey

In the vibrant hall of INS Shivaji, fresh batch of naval artificer trainees, all eager seventeen-year-olds with a penchant for the latest fashion, started their first day with morning briefing from training instructor, little did they anticipate that their sense of style was about to face a formidable adversary – the naval tradition of clean-shaven head, David-like haircuts.

After briefing, as the instruction sink in about the impending shearing session in afternoon, the trainees couldn't help but exchange anxious glances. Accustomed to their carefully nurtured hairstyles reminiscent of Bollywood stars like Amitabh Bachchan and Rajesh Khanna, the thought of parting with their beloved locks was met with a mixture of dread and amusement.

In the afternoon, with a sense of camaraderie that only a shared plight could foster, the trainees lined up outside the naval barber salon. One by one, they entered the salon with the swagger of a movie star, only to emerge moments later with a hairstyle reminiscent of the biblical David – short, practical, and starkly different from their previous glamorous selves.

The waiting trainees couldn't contain their laughter as each freshly shorn comrade joined the ranks of the closely cropped. The salon echoed with the sound of amusement, and the camaraderie among the trainees grew stronger with each transformation. The resemblance to David became so uncanny that, by late evening, the entire batch sported identical haircuts. As they looked at each other, sporting their new and uniform hairstyles, the initial shock transformed into uproarious laughter. The camaraderie that had blossomed in the face of a shared grooming experience forged a bond among the trainees that would last throughout their training.

Their introduction to naval life had started with a shearing session that turned their individualistic styles into a collective badge of companions. And as they stood side by side, heads held high, their uniformity became a symbol of the shared journey they were about to embark upon. Little did they know that those David-like haircuts would become a cherished memory, marking the beginning of a lifetime of shared stories and laughter among a group of trainees turned comrades.

The Initial Days

Vishal's and others initial days are a whirlwind of activities. They are issued uniforms, caps, shoes, boots, belts, winter clothing, sports clothing, sports shoes. Tailor was called in to take measurements for stitching white naval uniforms and ceremonial tunics. They check fittings of their uniform and introduce each other with greeting. The camaraderie among them is palpable, a shared sense of purpose binding them together. But beneath the surface lies an undercurrent of nervous energy as they await their first taste of training.

Trials of Endurance

The morning sun finds Vishal and his fellow trainees on the training grounds, sweat glistening on their brows as they push their bodies to the limit. From gruelling obstacle courses to intense endurance drills, they are put through their paces by the stern instructors. With each passing day, Vishal feels his muscles grow stronger and his determination deepen.

Military Discipline

In the barracks, Vishal learns the importance of military discipline although he had practiced it long as part of NCC training. From precise uniform inspections to marching drills, every aspect of their lives is governed by strict rules and regulations. But amidst the rigidity, Vishal finds a sense of pride in the discipline instilled within him, knowing that it will serve him well in the challenges ahead.

Navigating Academia

In the classroom, Vishal and others delves into the academic classes subject ranging from science, maths, and engineering drawings. The lessons of the past learning resonate within him, instilling a profound respect for the legacy he is now a part of.

Engineering Fundamentals

In the engineering classes, Vishal grapples with engineering drawing with complex equations and intricate designs. Three view plans and Isometric drawings were now regular part of their learnings. He immerses himself in the theoretical knowledge that will form the foundation of his future career. The challenges are daunting, but Vishal's passion for engineering drives him forward, determined to master the skills required of him.

A Beacon of Hope

As Vishal looks ahead to the next six months, he knows that the challenges will only grow more intense. But amidst the storm, he finds a beacon of hope in the knowledge that he is one step closer to realizing his dreams. With unwavering determination, he sets his sights on the horizon, ready to conquer whatever lies ahead on his journey to becoming a naval engineer.

Unity in Diversity: Challenges of Journey

In the training institute, as diverse group of young trainees from different corners of India found themselves thrown together in a whirlwind of excitement, challenges, and companionship, Vishal and others moved around onto the campus and barrack, greeted by unfamiliar faces, each one representing a unique cultural background and language. The air buzzed with the cadence of multiple languages – Marathi, Tamil, Punjabi, Malayalee and more – creating a rich tapestry of diversity that would come to define his training experience.

In the initial days, the language barrier seemed insurmountable. Vishal and many other struggled to communicate with his fellow trainees, often resorting to gestures and smiles to bridge the gap. The challenges were not only linguistic but cultural as well, as each trainee brought their own traditions and practices to the table. However, amidst the confusion and initial awkwardness, a shared goal emerged – the pursuit of excellence in naval training. As all engaged in rigorous physical exercises, learned naval tactics, and navigated the complexities of engineering, a sense of unity began to develop.

One evening, after a particularly challenging day, Vishal found himself sitting with a group of fellow trainees under the starlit sky. With a hint of hesitation, he mustered the courage to speak in English, a language that was foreign to many but served as the common ground they needed. He found few of the trainees were sons of retired or serving naval officers and had fair amount of naval knowledge and fluent English being product of Kendriya Vidyalaya.

"Today... tough day, no?" Vishal began tentatively, and soon, the floodgates opened. Others chimed in, sharing their thoughts, struggles, and triumphs in a mishmash of broken English. It wasn't perfect, but it was a start – a bridge that connected hearts across linguistic and cultural divides. In the following weeks, the trainees formed study groups, shared meals, and supported each other through the challenges of training. The barriers of language slowly crumbled, making way for a unique form of communication that blended accents, mispronunciations, and laughter.

As they spent more time together, the bonds strengthened. They discovered the richness of each other's cultures, shared stories from their hometowns, and even attempted to teach each other a few words in their native languages. The mess hall echoed with a cacophony of laughter and camaraderie that transcended linguistic differences. Vishal, reflecting on his journey, realized that the breaking of the language barrier had opened the door to a world of connections and understanding. The experience had taught him that, despite the diversity that surrounded him, the common language of friendship and shared purpose could overcome any obstacle.

Trainees Life- An Eventful Day

As new batch of naval artificer trainees embarked on a journey that would test their mettle and forge them into disciplined sailors. The day began with the blaring sound of a pipe whistle, signalling the start of the morning run led by a relentless physical trainer. Each day, at six in the morning, the trainees donned their PT uniforms, sipped their tea, and hit the ground running, the rhythmic thud of their footsteps echoing in the stillness of the morning. For some, the initial enthusiasm gave way to the harsh reality of physical exertion, leaving a few trainees struggling to keep up. The morning run was just the beginning. As the trainees returned to the barracks, breathless and perspiring, the physical trainer seamlessly transitioned them into gym training. Under the watchful eyes of seasoned instructors, the trainees learned to move as one cohesive unit, mastering the precision required for naval discipline.

After the breakfast, young trainees would gather in parade ground, in neatly pressed military rigs complete with boots and belt. Dress inspection would follow with march past and other naval drills. Hectic session would often leave trainees drained of energy by end of the period at tea break. Once the disperse is announced, all run for water and tea. Trainees proceeds for academic pursuits after tea break, their minds shifting from physical endurance to intellectual challenges. Post lunch, the trainees would again gather in classrooms, where nautical concepts, engineering principles, and naval procedures filled their notebooks as they delved into the academic rigors of naval training. Every Wednesday and Saturday afternoon was allocated for dress preparation from shining of boots, shoes, belt and buttons to preparing ceremonial uniform and so on. At the same time, this was the moment for little free chatter and fun.

But the day was far from over. As the clock ticked towards the sports time, the trainees braced themselves for another demanding session – boxing. Trainer would take them for another long countryside run across the hilly terrain around bushy dam. Once back and with gloves laced, they sparred with their fellow trainees, the sound of punches and the occasional groan filling the air. The boxing ring became a crucible where resilience and determination were tested, forging bonds of camaraderie among the trainees.

Evenings sports session was followed by a brief respite as all would get some time out to go market complex for refreshments and juice. Once back they all freshen up again after full day of hard work to proceed for the dinner in the dining mess.

Dinner was followed by evening self-studies to revisit their notes and textbooks. The seriousness of their commitment to their naval education became apparent. The weight of responsibility rested on their shoulders, and each trainee knew that success demanded both physical prowess and intellectual acumen. Before the lights-out call at ten in the night, the trainees retired to their bunks, their bodies weary, and minds filled with the day's experiences. In the dimly lit barracks, the rhythmic breathing of slumbering trainees marked the end of another arduous day.

As the weeks unfolded, some trainees faced injuries, and the medical inspection rooms became a frequent stop for those seeking solace for their aches and pains. Yet, dropping out was not an option – perseverance was the only path forward. The routine, initially daunting, became a crucible that tested the trainees' resolve, transforming them into a cohesive unit. As they overcame physical and mental challenges, the bond among the trainees grew stronger. They were bound by a shared commitment to becoming naval artificers, and each day of their rigorous routine brought them one step closer to that goal.

An Endurance Test- Pressure Retention

In the sun-drenched parade ground of INS Shivaji, where discipline was as sharp as the salutes, a moment of unexpected hilarity unfolded during a routine march past training session.

Dayal Mehra from Bombay, a young naval fellow trainee of Vishal, son of a retired naval officer, found himself in an increasingly desperate situation. Nature was calling with a persistence that even the rigid routines of naval training couldn't ignore. Ignoring the stern glances of his fellow trainees, he repeatedly whispered to the gunnery instructor, Balwant Singh, about the urgency of his situation.

"Sir! I really need to go, sir!" Dayal pleaded, hopping from one foot to the other in a comical attempt to contain the imminent disaster.

Balwant Singh, a seasoned instructor with a strict demeanour, tried to maintain his stern expression, but the urgency in Dayal's eyes was hard to ignore. However, Balwant Singh had his own sense of humour, and instead of granting Dayal permission immediately, he decided to test the limits of his endurance.

"Hold it, Dayal! Discipline comes first," Balwant Singh shouted in his deep, authoritative voice.

As the march past continued, the situation took a turn for the unexpected. The strain on Dayal's face reached a breaking point, and to the shock and amusement of everyone present, a trail of urine snaked its way across the parade ground, forming an impromptu path behind him. Realizing the gravity of the situation, Balwant Singh quickly changed his tone. "Run, Dayal! Get out of the parade ground!" he shouted, unable to suppress a chuckle.

Dayal, red-faced and mortified, made a hasty retreat while his fellow trainees struggled to maintain their military bearing, attempting to stifle laughter that threatened to erupt like a suppressed guffaw volcano. The incident became legendary among the trainees, a moment of levity in the otherwise regimented life at INS Shivaji. From that day forward, the mere mention of "Run Dayal" would send the trainees into fits of laughter, and Dayal, despite his initial embarrassment, learned to take it all in stride, becoming the unwitting hero of one of the most amusing episodes in the annals of naval training history.

An Unexpected Shot- Short Lived Freedom

In the tightly regimented life at INS Shivaji, where discipline and order were paramount, a group of artificer trainees in their first term, including Vishal, found themselves drawn into an unexpected escapade. Eager to break free from the monotony of their training routine, they hatched a plan to convince their training officer to allow them to go for a movie in institute's cinema hall, a privilege not yet granted to fresh trainees.

This group, mainly comprising trainees from the bustling cities of Delhi and Bombay, were known for their over-smart banter and lively spirits. Determined to create a memorable experience, they approached their training officer with a persuasive pitch, highlighting need for some change from routine mandarin. To their surprise, the training officer, swayed by their enthusiasm, granted them permission with a set of strict instructions to maintain decorum and uphold the discipline that was the hallmark of naval training.

Excitement filled the air as Vishal and his comrades, feeling a taste of freedom, entered the cinema hall. Little did they know that an unexpected incident would turn their outing into a memorable, albeit challenging chapter of their training. Prem, one of the trainees from Delhi, chose a moment during halftime to visit the restroom. Unfamiliar with the layout, he entered the officers' toilet instead of the trainees. Unaware of the mistake, he proceeded to use the facilities.

It was in that moment that an officer entered the restroom and confronted Prem about his presence in the officers' area. A spirited argument ensued, with Prem asserting to know what the difference is. Unaware to Prem, this exchange was reported to the training commander. The consequences were swift and severe. The entire group of trainees, including Vishal, found themselves facing collective punishment. The training commander, displeased with the breach of discipline, decided to halt movie privileges for the next three months, and surprisingly granted permission to other trainees with strict instruction. As the news of the collective punishment spread, Vishal and others learned a valuable lesson in responsibility and decorum. Despite their initial disappointment, they took the setback in stride, understanding the importance of adhering to the rules that governed their training.

In the months that followed, the incident became a humorous anecdote, a reminder that even in moments of leisure, the principles of discipline and respect for hierarchy must prevail. And while their movie outings were suspended, the experience served as a lasting lesson in the delicate balance between camaraderie and adherence to the stringent codes of naval life at INS Shivaji.

Bridging the Gap: Bonds Forged in Naval Engineering

In the institute, a tradition as old as the institution itself thrived, the passing of the torch from one batch of trainees to the next, creating a bond of camaraderie that transcended time and differences. With each new batch joining every six months, a cycle of disciplined ragging and grooming unfolded, shaping the lives of young naval engineering trainees, and fostering a sense of belonging that lasted a lifetime. By the end of their first term in campus, the trainees had become a tight-knit family, forever bound by the unique experience they had shared. As they bid farewell to first term to join the other senior trainees in different divisions in naval training institute, they carried with them skills needed to forge friendships in the crucible of diversity.

As the senior batch prepared to welcome the newcomers, excitement buzzed through the corridors of the institute. They meticulously planned their approach, eager to impart their wisdom and experiences to the incoming trainees while also testing their mettle through the age-old tradition of ragging. For the junior batch, the anticipation was palpable as they prepared to enter the hallowed halls of the institute. They had heard stories of the challenges that lay ahead - the rigorous training, the demanding schedules, and the daunting prospect of facing the scrutiny of their seniors. Yet, they were also eager to prove themselves and earn their place among their peers.

As Vishal's batch encountered with other senior batches, a whirlwind of activity ensued. The seniors, armed with a mix of mischief and mentorship, put the juniors through their paces, testing their knowledge, English language, their resilience, and their ability to think on their feet. But beneath the surface of the playful banter and good-natured teasing, there was a deeper purpose - to instil a sense of discipline, camaraderie, and mutual respect that would serve them well in their future careers as naval engineers.

Through the trials and tribulations of ragging, the bonds of friendship and camaraderie were forged. The seniors shared their experiences and imparted valuable lessons learned from their own time as junior trainees, while the juniors embraced the challenges with enthusiasm and determination, eager to prove themselves worthy of their mentor's trust and guidance.

As the months passed, the relationship between all the batches evolved from one of seniority and hierarchy to one of mutual respect and collaboration. The seniors took on the role of mentors, guiding their juniors through the intricacies of naval engineering and offering support and encouragement whenever needed. In turn, the juniors brought fresh perspectives and ideas to the table, invigorating the senior batch with their energy and enthusiasm. By the time the senior's term were ready to graduate and embark on their careers as naval engineers, the bonds they had formed with their junior counterparts were unbreakable. They had weathered the storms of training together, forged in the crucible of adversity, and emerged stronger and more resilient than ever.

As one by one each batch bid farewell to the institute every six months and set sail into the unknown, they carried with them not only the knowledge and skills they had acquired but also the memories of the friendships and camaraderie that had sustained them along the way. And though they may have left the training institute behind, the bonds they had forged with their junior counterparts would last a lifetime, a testament to the enduring spirit of camaraderie that defined their time as naval engineering trainees.

Forging Excellence: The Workshop Chronicles

In the majestic institute, Vishal soon found himself amidst the whirring of machinery and the scent of metal, surrounded by the cacophony of eager trainees. The workshops were a crucible of knowledge, where hands-on learning and practical applications transformed theoretical concepts into tangible skills.

Vishal, Udayan, Dayal, John, Ravi along with his diverse batch of fellow trainees, dove headfirst into the world of naval engineering workshops. Each day brought new challenges, and their instructors led them through a series of meticulously designed classes, each focusing on a specific aspect of engineering. The first workshop was dedicated to workshop practices of filing, machining, foundry, lathe shop, drilling machines, sheet metal work to welding, a skill that would be crucial in ensuring the structural integrity of naval vessels.

The first practical lesson of engineering for the trainees was in fitting workshop. Each trainee was given 50 mm round steel bar to turn it into a hexagon by chipping with the help of chisel-hammer and smoothening it by filing later. The practical lessons of fitting shop turned their delicate palms into bristles and hard skin.

As they progressed through the workshops, trainees learnt hydraulics. Each session was a puzzle to solve, a challenge to conquer, and a chance to push the boundaries of their knowledge. They discovered the value of teamwork, learning from each other's strengths and compensating for weaknesses.

In the later stage, they slowly delved into the awareness about the Steam and IC Engines, Gas Turbines, Propulsion systems and Pumps. Vishal, now acquainted with the sound of engines, learned the inner workings of marine propulsion, from traditional engines to the more complex machinery used in modern naval vessels. The class became a symphony of knowledge as trainees collaborated to solve problems and fine-tune their understanding.

The class on refrigeration and air conditioning introduced them to the mechanics and thermodynamics. Vishal, often accustomed to the hot summers of Delhi, now grasped the importance of climate control systems in ensuring the comfort and safety of those aboard a ship.

The workshops were not just about acquiring technical skills; they were a melting pot of ideas, cultures, and experiences. Vishal, with his unique perspective, contributed to the collective knowledge of the group. Amidst the clanger of machinery and the hum of activity, trainees shared not just knowledge but also laughter, frustrations, and triumphs. The workshops were more than a means to an end; they were the crucible in which these aspiring naval engineers were moulded into a cohesive unit, ready to face the challenges that lay ahead on the high seas.

Balancing Steel and Dreams: Yearning for Youth

In training base, young trainees, all in their late teens, were immersed in a world of discipline, duty, and naval protocol. As they pursued their dreams of serving the nation, the juxtaposition of their military training against the vibrant and carefree lives they once knew brought a poignant ache for the civil life they had temporarily left behind.

Vishal, a 17-year-old now was with dreams as vast as the ocean. As the days unfolded within the confines of the naval base, Vishal and his peers couldn't help but yearn for the civil life they had temporarily put on hold. They missed the laughter echoing through college corridors, the spontaneity of weekend plans, and the friendships shared over fast foods and movies. They all felt home sick, missed home cooked food, and would often remember good old days of school time eating at corner joints. The contrast between their disciplined naval routine and the carefree activities of their civilian counterparts began to weigh on the young trainees. In the evenings, instead of hanging out with friends at local cafes or attending music event, they found themselves engaged in intense physical training, sports, military drills, and classes on naval technology.

As the weekends approached, the trainees longed for a taste of the civil life they had momentarily left behind. They yearned for the freedom to explore the city, attend social gatherings, and partake in the kind of leisure activities their peers in the civilian world enjoyed. Vishal often found himself reminiscing about the carefree days of school and college, where weekends were marked by impromptu trips, or visiting market of Connaught Place, South Extension and evenings spent with friend under the starlit sky. The friendship they once shared had been replaced by the structured discipline of the naval base, leaving a void that even the tightest bonds among the trainees couldn't entirely fill.

Despite the yearning for the civil life they missed, the young trainees knew that their sacrifice was a necessary stepping stone toward achieving their dreams. They found solace in the shared aspirations of their fellow comrades, bonding over the challenges they faced and the dreams that fuelled their journey. As the months passed, Vishal and his peers discovered the resilience within themselves. The yearning for the civil life transformed into a motivation to excel in their training. They learned to appreciate the sense of duty and discipline instilled by their naval instructors, recognizing that it was shaping them into strong, capable individuals ready to face the challenges of serving in the navy.

As they progressed in their training, the balance between the discipline of naval life and the yearning for the civil life became a part of their narrative. After three months, fresh trainees were now allowed to visit Lonavala market in their white naval uniform on Sunday. The companionships they forged within the naval base, coupled with the memories of their civilian lives, shaped them into well-rounded individuals, ready to navigate both the structured seas of naval service and the free-flowing currents of civilian life once their training was complete.

Echoes of Rebellion: An Unexpected Night at Training Institute

On completion of first semester term, Vishal's batch in a group of five each, was distributed among different accommodation blocks of trainees, creating a diverse tapestry of naval trainees mixed in Korigarh, Hemgarh, Narayangarh, Sudhagarh, Raigarh and Lohagarh divisions. Discipline and order were the guiding principles here. New batch was under strict surveillance of seniors and were picked for punishment often over slightest of mistake. Vishal and others found themselves thrust into the midst of an unexpected and tumultuous one night.

On an ordinary evening, during their daily routine inspection of accommodation block at 9 pm, the Duty Lieutenant Commander (DLC), a stern figure with years of naval experience, once crossed Raigarh division and reached little away, he suddenly found himself under a barrage of stone pelting. Chaos erupted as the unexpected assault sent shockwaves through the training grounds. The night, which had started like any other, took an unforeseen turn. The DLC, undeterred by the unexpected assault, swiftly mobilized the trainee authorities. Interrogations ensued, with the entire parade ground becoming a scene of intense scrutiny. Vishal and his fellow trainees, initially bewildered by the turn of events, were soon caught up in the wave of investigations.

As the night wore on, the trainee authorities took a no-nonsense approach. Punishments were meted out, and the parade ground became a place of collective accountability for all artificer trainees. The harsh disciplinary measures extended until two am, leaving the trainees physically exhausted and mentally drained. Amid the stern voices and commands echoing in the night, six suspects emerged. Pointed out as the potential instigators of the stone pelting incident, they were promptly confined to a cell for further investigation. The once-unified block now bore the scars of an unexpected indiscipline, and the consequences were severe.

The confined cell became a temporary home for the suspected trainees, their actions shrouded in mystery and the repercussions looming large. The atmosphere within the training institute was charged with tension, as rumours and speculation circulated among the trainees. The unexpected act of defiance had shattered the usual order, leaving everyone on edge. In the days that followed, investigations continued, and the naval authorities sought to uncover the motives behind the act of rebellion. The training institute, usually a bastion of discipline and camaraderie, grappled with the aftermath of the stone pelting incident. The action had cast a shadow over the entire artificer community.

As Vishal and his fellow trainees navigated the repercussions of that tumultuous night, they came to realize the fragile balance that existed within the tightly knit naval training community. The incident served as a stark reminder that, even in the structured world of military discipline, the undercurrents of discontent could erupt unexpectedly, leaving a lasting impact on the journey of every trainee within those hallowed walls.

Collective Solidarity and Camaraderie

In INS Shivaji, a unique partnership flourished among the naval artificer trainees. The bonds they forged went beyond the routine of drills and lectures, creating a brotherhood that would be tested one fateful evening. It was on display when a group of senior trainees found themselves confined to cells as a collective punishment for a stone-pelting incident targeting duty commander during the evening inspection. The trainees watched in silence as their senior partner were led away, uncertainty clouding their faces. In the confined cells, instead of resentment, a spirit of solidarity blossomed among the trainees. Far from being downtrodden, they saw an opportunity to turn the situation into a statement of unity. Their cells became a hub of whispered conversations and shared laughter, transforming the confines into a makeshift haven.

As word spread among the other trainees about the collective punishment, a wave of support surged among artificer trainees through INS Shivaji. The unsung heroes in confinement became a symbol of solidarity against the disciplinary action. To show their empathy, trainees from all batches found subtle ways to express their support. From covert nods of encouragement during drills to coded messages passed in the mess hall, the unity among the trainees became palpable.

The mess in charge, a senior artificer trainee in his third year, noticed the undercurrent of partners. Realizing that the confined trainees were becoming accidental heroes, he decided to make a subtle gesture of support. Special meals, handpicked by the mess in charge himself, were delivered to the cells of the confined trainees. The aroma of the carefully crafted meals wafted through the confined space, eliciting smiles from the trainees within. The gesture wasn't just about food; it was a symbol of the solidarity that transcended the disciplinary boundaries imposed on them. As the confined trainees enjoyed their special meals, the mess in charge's message was clear – they weren't forgotten or abandoned.

The confined trainees, instead of feeling isolated, became beacons of unity. The silent protest against the perceived injustice brought all trainees together. Each day, as the sun dipped below the horizon, the unsung heroes in the cells found solace in the partnership that flourished within their confined space.

Vishal, along with a handful of other junior trainees, experienced the peculiar rhythm of night duty as part of training. Assigned the late-night shift from two to six in the morning, they patrolled the cell corridors with a sense of responsibility, knowing that the confined seniors were in their cells, serving out their punishment. In the quiet hours of the night,

Vishal and other companions approached the cells for duty. However, as the night wore and the monotony of the patrol set in, they felt asleep and frequently dosed off sitting outside.

With a sly understanding, a deal was suggested to them by the confined seniors. The junior on duty trainees would take turns sleeping inside the cells, providing a brief respite, all this while confined seniors roamed outside the cell freely. The clandestine exchange became a routine during the late-night shifts. In those stolen moments, Vishal and his companions experienced a sense of rebellion, a subtle defiance against the rigid structure of military discipline. They took turns catching a few moments of much-needed rest within the confines of the cells, knowing that they had to be vigilant when the patrol approached at six in the morning for their routine inspection. As the week passed, the arrangement became a well-orchestrated dance, a silent understanding between the confined seniors and the junior trainees on sentry duty. The night watch became not just a duty but a shared experience, a small act of camaraderie amid the discipline of naval training.

When the confined seniors completed their punishment, the clandestine exchanges ceased, and life at INS Shivaji returned to its usual rhythm. The late-night escapades became a secret shared among the junior and senior trainees, a tale that added a touch of mischief to their memories of training at the naval institute. In the end, the nighttime exchanges served as a reminder that even in the structured environment of military training, bonds of partnership and creativity could flourish, turning a seemingly mundane duty into an unforgettable chapter in the shared history of naval artificer trainees at INS Shivaji.

When their confinement period ended, and punishment converted into fourteen days of harsh physical drill every day, the senior trainees emerged not as rebels, but as symbols of unity and resilience. Their story became a whispered legend among the trainees of INS Shivaji, a reminder that even in the face of adversity, the bonds of comradeship could withstand the harshest storms. As the training continued, the legacy of the confined heroes lived on, a testament to the strength that flourished when naval artificer trainees stood shoulder to shoulder, united in their pursuit of excellence on the shores of INS Shivaji.

The Wide Arena of Sports

In the surroundings of INS Shivaji, where the rigorous training of naval artificers unfolded, the importance of physical fitness was emphasized alongside academic and technical excellence. The naval artificer trainees, fresh-faced and eager, found themselves immersed in a world of outdoor sports that became an integral part of their training routine.

As the weeks progressed, the trainees would disperse to different sporting arenas during their allotted sports periods. Some would sprint across the football field, their cleats digging into the soft earth as they honed their skills and teamwork. Meanwhile, others would weave their way through the hockey field, the resounding thud of the ball against the stick echoing in the air.

The basketball court would come alive with the rhythmic bounce of the ball and the squeak of rubber soles as trainees engaged in fast-paced games, showcasing their agility and strategic thinking. For those seeking the refreshing embrace of water, the swimming pool became a sanctuary where strokes and dives were perfected under the watchful eye of instructors.

On weekends, the sports complex transformed into a hub of activity. Cricket matches unfolded on the green fields, the crack of the bat and the shouts of encouragement creating a lively atmosphere. Indoors, snooker sessions and table tennis matches added a touch of competitive camaraderie to the ante room. Sports served as more than just a recreational outlet for the trainees; it became a means of fostering teamwork, discipline, and physical endurance. The institute's sports facilities not only kept them motivated but also provided a much-needed break from the intensity of their training sessions.

As the trainees honed their skills, a select few stood out, earning the opportunity to represent INS Shivaji in various tournaments. Some would proudly wear the institute's colours in inter-command competitions, while others, displaying exceptional prowess, went on to participate in inter-services tournaments, showcasing the talent that had been cultivated during their training.

Beyond the physical benefits, sports became a unifying force among the trainees. The bonds forged on the field translated into a sense of camaraderie that extended beyond the realm of sports. Whether facing off in a cricket match or battling for supremacy on the basketball court, the trainees of INS Shivaji discovered the enduring power of sports in shaping both their physical and interpersonal skills.

Glimpse of Glamour and Charm

In the confined world of INS Shivaji, the prospect of any interaction with the girls was a rare and eagerly awaited occurrence. Among the trainees, most of whom were in their teens, the sports sessions held a special allure, offering a brief respite from the structured environment. As the shrill whistle echoed across the sports grounds, signalling the start of the sports session, a palpable excitement buzzed through the air. The trainees, clad in their sports gear, eagerly assembled on the field, ready for a break from the rigors of naval training. However, it wasn't just the thrill of athletic competition that fuelled their enthusiasm; it was the prospect of catching a glimpse of the young girls who occasionally graced the play area. These girls were mostly the daughters of the institute's officers and staff, and their presence was a rare and cherished sight for the trainees who were otherwise deprived of such possibilities.

Post-sports session, the market area near the institute became a hub of activity. Trainees would venture there for a well-deserved break, relishing the opportunity to indulge in snacks and treats. It was during these moments that the young girls, perhaps sensing the trainees' eagerness, would often be seen in the vicinity. Innocent antics unfolded at times as the trainees tried to catch the attention of the girls. Laughter echoed through the market area as jokes were exchanged, and playful banter filled the air. The girls, in turn, enjoyed the attention, appreciating the light-hearted interactions with the trainees. For those brief moments, the rigid barriers of military life softened, allowing the trainees to experience a sense of normalcy and youthful exuberance. The shared laughter, the friendly exchanges, and the joy of simple companionship offered a welcome break from the intensity of their training routine.

As the sun dipped below the horizon, signalling the end of their recreation time, the trainees returned to the structured world of INS Shivaji, their hearts a little lighter from the fleeting moments of connection with the opposite sex. These innocent encounters became cherished memories, a source of joy, and a reminder that even in the disciplined life of naval training, the human spirit yearns for moments of joy and thrill.

Tides of Change: A Bittersweet Farewell

By now, Vishal and his other trainees had formed an unbreakable bond forged by shared experiences, challenges, and triumphs. For a whole year, they had stood side by side, navigating the intricacies of marine and mechanical engineering together. But now, as the time came for some of them to part ways, the air was tinged with a bittersweet mix of excitement and sorrow.

Vishal has longed for Marine Engineering course as his preferred stream, but fate had already decided next course for him. Among those leaving was Vishal, Arjun, Pradeep, Jagdeesh, Ravinder and Rajat, who had been selected to pursue training as Shipwright Artificer in the Ship Construction and Naval Architecture at another institute in Bombay. As the news spread, a palpable sense of heartbreak swept through the group, their tight-knit circle suddenly fractured by the looming separation.

Vishal, Arjun, Pradeep, Jagdeesh, Ravinder and Rajat, and the rest of their friends gathered in their dormitory, their faces etched with sadness as they contemplated the impending farewell. Memories of late-night study sessions, impromptu football and hockey matches, and shared laughter flooded their minds, each moment a testament to the bond they had formed over the past year. As they sat in silence, grappling with the reality of their impending separation, Vishal couldn't help but feel a knot form in his stomach. Udayan, his closest friend, had been his constant companion throughout their time at the institute, offering support and encouragement when the workload seemed overwhelming.

Salil and John, too, had become like family to Vishal, their friendship a source of strength and comfort in times of uncertainty. The thought of saying goodbye to them felt like losing a piece of himself, a void that could never be filled. But amidst the sorrow, there was also a sense of pride and excitement for their friend's future endeavours. The Naval Construction branch was a prestigious opportunity, one that promised new challenges and adventures on the horizon. As much as Udayan and the others would miss them, they knew that this was an opportunity they couldn't pass up.

And so, as the day of departure arrived, Udayan and other batchmate gathered one last time to bid farewell to Vishal and others. Tears flowed freely as they embraced, their hearts heavy with the weight of goodbye. But beneath the surface, there was a flicker of hope - hope for the future, hope for reunion, and hope that their friendship would endure, no matter the distance that separated them.

As Vishal and others boarded the train bound for their new institute at Bombay, Udayan and Salil watched with a mixture of sadness and pride. They may be parting ways for now, but their bond was unbreakable, anchored by the memories they had shared and the friendship that would carry them through whatever challenges lay ahead. And as the train disappeared into the distance, Vishal knew that this was not the end, but merely the beginning of a new chapter in their journey together.

Navigating Waves and Wonders: A Shipwright's Tale in Bombay

In the heart of Bombay, amidst the bustling streets and towering skyscrapers, a cohort of young navy shipwright trainees found themselves embarking on the next phase of their maritime journey. Aged around 18 years, these eager minds had completed their initial year of training at Lonavala and now stood at the threshold of a specialized institute for Ship Construction and Naval Architecture.

The Shipwright Training Institute in Bombay welcomed these young enthusiasts, introducing them to a world where the intricacies of ship design and construction would become their playground for the next three years. As the trainees settled into their new surroundings, camaraderie blossomed among them, forming bonds that would last a lifetime. Following the footstep of preceding five batches, the new trainees navigate through their specialized courses, delving into the complexities of naval architecture and ship construction. From classrooms to shipyards, the institute provided a comprehensive learning environment where theoretical knowledge met hands-on experience.

Weekdays were dedicated to rigorous academic pursuits, where the trainees immersed themselves in engineering and ship drawings, naval architecture principles, structural analysis, ship technology, ship stability, ship systems, marine engineering and the skill and artistry of ship and boat design. In the shipyard, they got their hands dirty, learning the nuances of constructing and assembling vessels over the period of entire training, under the watchful eyes of seasoned instructors. At the Institute, at beginning trainees were led through the process of boat building. They would carve out wooden planks as per drawings, learn seasoning process, bending of wood, caulking, and creating wooden joints marked their joinery journey. Each batch in their third semester would partly contribute to complete the skeleton of a whaler boat in the making at Institute. Practical classes in forging, sheet metal work, piping, gas and arc welding, FRP boat work followed as training progressed.

Their days were filled with excitement and anticipation as they made regular visits to the Mazagaon Dock Limited and the Naval Dockyard at Bombay as part of their classes. These visits weren't just routine tasks; they were opportunities to delve into the intricacies of shipbuilding, to witness firsthand the craftsmanship and expertise that went into constructing the vessels that sailed the seas. Amidst the cacophony of shipyard activities and the rhythmic clang of metal against metal, Vishal and his batch of trainees in ship construction and Naval Architecture, embarked on a journey of discovery and learning. As they strolled through the workshops, Vishal and others were fascinated by the diversity of skills at play – from the intricate welding of steel plates to the meticulous installation of complex machinery. The shipwright trainees were not just observers; they actively engaged with the craftsmen, asking questions, and participating in hands-on experiences.

Heavy steel fabrications and welding, plate cutting machines, paintings, outfitting workshops, shafting & propellers, machineries and ship equipment, piping shops, drydocks, slipways, building berth gave them the glimpses of what it takes to build a naval ship. At the shop floors of the shipyards, Vishal and his batch mate were greeted by a symphony of sounds and sights. Everywhere they looked, there were men hard at work, their hands moving with precision and skill as they welded, riveted, and assembled the massive steel structures that would eventually become ships.

The design offices were large halls filled with drawing boards and draftsman hovering over drawing lines on tracing sheets. The ammonia printing on papers from tracings and the smell of ammonia, papers cutting strewn all over was a new experience altogether. Under the guidance of seasoned shipbuilders and naval architects, Vishal and his batch mate absorbed every detail, eagerly soaking up the wealth of knowledge that surrounded them. From the layout of the shipyard to the intricacies of hull design, they learned the importance of attention to detail and meticulous planning in the shipbuilding process.

Their visits to the Mazagaon Dock Ltd and the Naval Dockyard were not just educational; they were transformative experiences that shaped their understanding of the maritime industry. They gained a newfound appreciation for the collaborative effort that went into building a ship, from the initial design stages to the final touches before launch. As they wandered the shop floors, Vishal and his batch mate struck up conversations with the workers and engineers, eager to learn from their experiences and insights. They listened intently as tales of maritime adventures and shipbuilding challenges were shared, gaining valuable perspectives that would stay with them throughout their careers.

With each visit, Vishal and his batch mate grew mentally richer, their passion for shipbuilding and naval architecture burning brighter than ever before. They knew that they were embarking on a journey that would take them to the farthest reaches of the seas, and they were determined to make the most of every opportunity that came their way.

As they bid farewell to the shipyard training at Bombay, Vishal and his batch mate carried with them not just memories, but a newfound sense of purpose and determination. They knew that they were destined for greatness in the world of shipbuilding, and they were ready to set sail on their journey towards success.

Fun and Play in the Street of Bombay.

But it wasn't all work and no play for the young trainees. During weekends, they would venture out into the vibrant streets of Bombay, exploring its myriad attractions and soaking in the city's vibrant culture. From visiting iconic landmarks like the Gateway of India and Marine Drive to sampling street food delicacies at bustling markets, they embraced the hustle and bustle of city life with enthusiasm and curiosity.

Back at the Shipwright Training institute, camaraderie flourished among the trainees, as they formed tight-knit bonds forged through shared experiences and mutual interests. Whether they were working together on class projects, playing sports on the institute's ground, or simply hanging out in the common areas, laughter and friendship were always in abundance.

The dining mess was the place where during mealtime, all senior or junior exchanged views and sought guidance. Bachan Singh, a man in his fifties, who worked in mess close to thirty years by now, had fed and served every shipwright trainee like his own child, and looked after their needs. He would occasionally tell the tales of those seniors who have long left to serve on the ship or have left the navy by now. Every trainee regarded him with utmost respect for his affection and care.

The weekend cricket matches played at Navy Nagar ground while packed lunch came from mess, Sunday's cross-country race from Institute in Fort area to Navy Nagar and back through Cuffe parade was a regular activity. Daily morning run to Marine Lines or hockey matches in Cross Maidan were part of their routine activities unlike for their other trade counterparts training at remote but picturesque Lonavala or the Jamnagar.

However, weekends ushered in a different rhythm to their lives. The vibrant city of Bombay became their playground, offering a plethora of experiences waiting to be explored. The trainees eagerly embraced the cultural diversity and bustling energy of the city, often spending weekends in joyful exploration. From Marine Drive's mesmerizing sunset views to the chaotic yet enchanting markets of Colaba, the trainees soaked in the city's charm. Navigating local trains, exploring street food, watching movies and absorbing the rich history at iconic landmarks like the Gateway of India, Flora Fountain, Horniman Circle, Asiatic Library, Fort area and Ballard Estate, generally deserted on Sundays, became weekend traditions. Occasionally, they witnessed film shooting and glimpses of film star in the area which often took place there. The city, with its vibrant tapestry, provided the perfect backdrop for the trainees to unwind and forge friendships that transcended the confines of their training institute.

Sports arenas echoed with their laughter as they engaged in friendly matches, fostering a spirit of healthy competition and camaraderie. As the trainees progressed through their years in Bombay, they not only honed their technical skills but also matured into a cohesive unit, each contributing their unique strengths to the collective learning experience. The city's energy mirrored their journey – fast-paced, dynamic, and filled with the promise of new horizons.

In the shipyard and classrooms, they laid the foundation for their future careers. On the streets of Bombay, they discovered the pulse of the country and the resilience that would define their naval careers. And so, under the watchful gaze of the Gateway of India, these young shipwright trainees continued to navigate the waves of knowledge and wonder, embracing the transformative journey that lay ahead.

Naval Training

Military Training at Firing Range

Trainees Cricket Team at Bombay **Post Cross Country Race at Bombay**

Young Naval Trainees at Bombay **On the way to Elephanta Caves on boat**

An Altercation- Questioning of Authority

Vishal, by now was a senior trainee after two years at the Shipwright Training Institute, found himself in an unexpected role during his second last semester. As the Trainee Petty Officer, he was responsible for overseeing the welfare and discipline of his fellow trainees. Little did he know that his leadership skills would be put to the test in a way he never anticipated.

It was the beginning of January 1981, and as per the institute's tradition, cabin reassignments were underway for the new semester. Trainees from various naval backgrounds were accustomed to this routine, but tensions rose unexpectedly when the trainees from the Sri Lankan navy objected to their new cabin allocations. Vishal, trying to maintain order, attempted to reason with the Sri Lankan trainees, explaining that the cabin assignments were made fairly and according to protocol. However, his efforts were met with defiance, and one Sri Lankan trainee, Pareira, resorted to physical aggression, pushing Vishal in the midst of the argument.

The insult to Vishal's authority didn't sit well with many of the Indian trainees, and tempers flared. What started as a disagreement quickly escalated into a heated altercation, with fists flying and voices raised in anger. In the chaos, the Sri Lankan trainees sought refuge with the duty officer, seeking protection from the escalating confrontation. The institute's authorities swiftly intervened, and disciplinary action was taken against the Sri Lankan as well as few Indian trainees, in accordance with to rules and regulations. Punishments were meted out, serving as a stern reminder of the importance of respecting authority and maintaining discipline within the institute.

In the aftermath of the incident, tensions simmered down, and a sense of normalcy gradually returned to the institute. Despite the initial strife, the trainees from different backgrounds eventually found common ground and continued to live and work together as they had before. The otherwise, relations among Indian, Sri Lankan and from African Nation such as Nigerian, Ghana or Tanzanian had mostly been cordial, occasionally hot, and cold due to cultural differences. Vishal in past had even hosted Sri Lankan and Nigerian friends at his house when they visited for sightseeing Delhi during annual leave.

The incident served as a learning experience for all, reinforcing the importance of mutual respect, understanding, and unity among trainees, regardless of their nationality or background. And for Vishal, it was a lesson in leadership and conflict resolution that would stay with him throughout his naval career.

Home Away from Home

Vishal, young and ambitious, found himself at a crossroads after he left the serene surroundings of Lonavala and ventured into the bustling city of Bombay for his naval architecture training. The shift had marked a significant change in his life, and with it came the bittersweet experience of parting with his close friend and batchmate, Udayan.

The city, with its vibrant energy, was a stark contrast to the quietude of Lonavala. However, the absence of Udayan by his side left a void that echoed the friendship they had shared during their training days. Despite the geographical separation, Vishal was determined to keep the bonds of friendship alive. Udayan's parents, who lived in a Bombay suburb, became a surrogate family for Vishal. Every month, without fail, he would make the journey to visit them, seeking solace in the familiarity of their company. The warmth of their home and the affectionate embrace of Udayan's parents provided a sense of belonging that eased the homesickness Vishal felt for his own family in Delhi. Vishal would share stories of their training days with Udayan's parents, recounting the challenges and triumphs they faced together.

Over time, the monthly visits became a cherished ritual. Udayan's parents, having embraced Vishal as one of their own, delighted in his company. Vishal, in turn, found a home away from home, a place where the laughter and memories of his training days echoed through the corridors. He loved the south Indian food prepared by Udyan's mother every time he visited them and would always return only after dinner back to training institute at Fort.

As Vishal navigated the complexities of naval architecture training, he drew strength from the support of Udayan's parents. Their encouragement and unconditional love fuelled his determination to excel in his chosen field. The visits not only served as a bridge connecting the past with the present but also as a testament to the enduring power of friendship.

Amid the challenges posed by naval architecture training, Vishal discovered that true bonds could withstand the test of distance. Udayan's parents, with their open hearts and welcoming home, played a pivotal role in helping Vishal create a support system that complemented the camaraderie he had experienced in Lonavala. And as the months unfolded, Vishal's journey in Bombay became not just a chapter in his naval training but a poignant tale of friendship, resilience, and the unwavering ties that bind hearts across the miles.

Sports- A Breather from Training

Vishal, a young and enthusiastic naval trainee, was immersed in the world of sports during his time at the Shipwright Training Institute in Bombay. Blessed with a natural talent for hockey, Vishal caught the eye of his trainers and peers during inter-command matches among institutes, ships, and other units within the Western Naval Command.

As part of a select few from the institute, Vishal, Ishwar, Shiv, Prem and Balbir were chosen to represent the Western Naval Command hockey team in an upcoming tournament. Excitement buzzed through the air as Vishal and his teammates geared up for the challenge ahead. Every day, they would gather on the field for rigorous practice sessions at Navy Nagar ground, honing their skills and fine-tuning their teamwork. Under the guidance of their coaches, they worked tirelessly, striving to reach their peak performance for the tournament.

Finally, the day of the Navy tournament arrived, and the Western Naval Command hockey team geared up for the competition. The Navy championship was being played at Cochin. Vishal and his teammates donned their navy-blue jerseys with pride, ready to showcase their talent on the hockey field. The competition was fierce, with teams from across the Navy vying for victory. Despite being trainees, they held their own, displaying remarkable skill and determination. They played with heart and passion, leaving everything they had on the field. Their hard work paid off as they advanced through the tournament, earning accolades for their impressive performance. But their journey came to an unexpected halt. As trainees, they were faced with the reality of their commitments. The demands of their rigorous training schedules meant that they could not afford the long absences required to continue playing for the services.

With heavy hearts, Vishal and his trainee teammates bid farewell to the hockey field, their dreams of representing the Navy at a higher-level put-on hold. Though they may not have been able to pursue their hockey careers further, the memories of their time on the field together would remain etched in their minds forever. Despite the disappointment, Vishal and his teammates took solace in the bonds they had formed through their shared love of the game. And though their hockey journey may have been cut short, they knew that the lessons they had learned and the experiences they had gained would stay with them for a lifetime.

Navigating Waves of Change: The Relocation to Vizag

In the early of 1981, a wave of change swept the naval training establishment for Ship Construction and Naval Architecture in Bombay. The decision had been made to relocate the entire institute to Vizag, on completion of semester in Jun 1981, a larger complex area with more space and resources, but far removed from the charm and familiarity of Bombay city. For the naval trainees, instructors, and management alike, the relocation brought forth a myriad of intricacies and challenges.

As the news of the relocation spread, the trainees found themselves grappling with mixed emotions. While excited about the prospect of new facilities and opportunities in Vizag, they couldn't help but feel a sense of nostalgia for the vibrant streets and bustling culture of Bombay. Leaving behind the city that had become their home for the past few years was no easy feat. For the instructors and naval management, the relocation presented a logistical puzzle of epic proportions. Coordinating the transfer of equipment, materials, and personnel from Bombay to Vizag was a herculean task, requiring meticulous planning and coordination. The logistics of relocating an entire training establishment were daunting, to say the least.

Amidst the chaos of packing and preparation, there was an air of uncertainty and apprehension among the trainees. Would the new facilities in Vizag live up to their expectations? Would they be able to adjust to life in a new city, far away from the comforts of home? These questions lingered in their minds as they bid farewell to Bombay and embarked on the journey to their new training grounds.

Arriving in Vizag, the trainees were greeted by the sight of vast expanses of open land and sprawling training facilities some still under development. Vishal's was the seniormost batch among six trainee batches, who had moved from Bombay to the new establishment, will now be trained here and the first to pass out from here. While impressed by the scale of their new surroundings, they couldn't help but feel a pang of homesickness for the familiar sights and sounds of Bombay. Adjusting to life in a new city proved to be a challenge, as they navigated the intricacies of Vizag's culture and customs.

Meanwhile, the instructors and naval management worked tirelessly to ensure a smooth transition for the trainees. From setting up classrooms and workshops to organizing orientation programs and recreational activities, they spared no effort in making the newcomers feel welcome and at home in their new environment. Creating of a green environment and surrounding full of trees and plants was a task all were committed to.

Despite the initial challenges and adjustments, the relocation to Vizag proved to be a transformative experience for the trainees. Over time, they grew accustomed to their new surroundings, forging bonds of camaraderie and resilience that would last a lifetime. The training at Mazagaon Dock Ltd, Bombay was replaced with training at Hindustan Shipyard Ltd., Vishakhapatnam while training workshops of Naval Dockyard, Bombay were replaced by Naval Dockyard, Vizag. And as they immersed themselves in their training, they realized that while the location may have changed, their passion for naval architecture and ship construction remained unwavering. And as they looked towards the future, they knew that no matter where their training took them, they would always carry with them the lessons learned and memories forged during their time in Vizag.

New institute was headed by highly accomplished Captain Collins, a shipwright officer of repute as its new officer in Charge. The institute slowly grew later to be commissioned as INS Vishwakarma in line with INS Shivaji, INS Valsura and INS Garuda.

Wired for Success: The Naval Electrical Artificer's Journey

The batch of seventy new aspiring electrical artificer engineers had arrived at INS Valsura, Jamnagar in end January 1978, after their selection at Lonavala. They embarked on a transformative journey as their four-year Naval Electrical Artificer training commenced. Among them was Ashok Kaushal from Delhi, a young man with a passion for all things electrical, ready to immerse himself in the world of naval technology.

The first year unfolded as a whirlwind of theoretical classes and practical exercises. Ashok, Pardesi, David, Francis, Negi, Prem, Chander Shekhar, Raj and other trainees delved into the fundamentals of electrical engineering, studying everything from circuitry to electronic components. The classrooms buzzed with the sound of eager minds absorbing the intricacies of their chosen field.

As the second year approached, the trainees transitioned from the classroom to hands-on training in state-of-the-art laboratories. They tinkered with electrical equipment, troubleshooting faults, and mastering the art of preventive maintenance and learnt about power generation and distributions, Control systems, motors, AC and DC power, power converters, ships electrical equipment. Under the guidance of experienced instructors, they gained practical insights into the challenges awaiting them in the fleet.

The start of third year training marked a deeper dive into practical areas of naval electrical systems. All trainees had to undertake six months afloat training on board naval ships. They had to undergo three months each on two ships to get acquainted with ships electrical technology. Living aboard naval vessels, they grappled with real-world challenges, fine-tuning electrical systems amidst the rhythmic roll of the waves. It was a period of intense learning, where theory met practice in the unforgiving environment of the open sea.

Trainees like of Ashok and others found themselves self-captivated by the complexities of shipboard power generation, distribution, and switch boards; others were either gearing up for Propulsion and other machinery control systems; or Navigation systems such as Radars, Echo Sounder, Speed Logs; Communication system MF/HF radios, satellite communication, Weapon engineering and control system, and advanced surveillance systems used on naval ships. Simulations and practical training exercises prepared them for the dynamic environment they would soon encounter in the naval fleet.

As they returned to Valsura after six months for remaining course of on and half years, electrical artificer were distributed in two different streams for specialisation. One called A-stream for the European origin ship while C-stream specialised in Russian ship technology. Trainees were additionally divided for further specialisation in stream such as Power, Controls and Radio Communication. In the final semester of six months, all C-stream trainees left for INS Satvahana for specialisation.

Throughout their four-year journey, Ashok and his fellow trainees forged bonds that transcended mere camaraderie. They became a close-knit community, supporting each other through the rigors of training, sharing victories, and weathering challenges together. The friendships formed during late-night study sessions and hands-on experiments became a crucial part of their shared experience.

As the day of graduation approached, the trainees looked back at the four years with a sense of accomplishment and nostalgia. They had transformed from eager novices to skilled naval artificers, ready to serve their country with expertise and dedication. The bonds formed at INS Valsura would continue to anchor them, even as they embarked on diverse paths within the naval fleet.

Ashok, along Pardesi, David, Francis, Negi, Prem, Chander Shekhar, Raj and other batchmate trainees were now a qualified Naval Electrical

Artificer Engineers, stood tall at the facilitation ceremony. The sea breeze carried a promise of new horizons, and he and his friends knew that their journey was far from over. With their training complete, they were ready to step into the challenges that awaited them in the vast expanse of the Indian Ocean, armed with knowledge, camaraderie, and a shared commitment to excellence. He was now ready to experience the on-work intricacies of his entire learning on ships where he was to join and meet and work together with his other counterparts from Marine Engineering, Ship Construction & Naval Architecture and the Aeronautical engineers including Electrical Aeronautical.

Skyward Bound: The Wings of Naval Artificer

After completing two years of foundational training at INS Shivaji and INS Valsura, all aviation artificer engineers honed their further skills in training institute at INS Garuda, the naval training establishment specializing in aviation engineering at Cochin. Varun, an electrical aviation artificer has moved from INS Valsura and joined Garuda training base. Varun and others naval artificers, batchmate of Ashok, were at a new juncture in their careers as they joined INS Garuda. Unfortunately, in this semester there was none for the mechanical aviation training, so no one joined from INS Shivaji.

The sprawling campus of INS Garuda, at Willingdon Island nestled along the coast of Cochin, echoed with the hum of aircraft and the buzz of eager trainees ready to take flight in their careers. The Air Aviation branch offered a unique set of challenges and opportunities, and Varun couldn't help but feel a mix of excitement and anticipation as he stepped into this new phase of training.

The initial months were dedicated to theoretical aspects of aircraft engineering, avionics systems, and the intricacies of maintaining and repairing naval aircraft. Varun along with his other peers underwent rigorous classroom sessions, absorbing knowledge from experienced instructors who had themselves soared through the skies in service to the Indian Navy.

As the training progressed, the focus shifted towards hands-on experiences. The trainees found themselves working on actual aircraft, learning the art of diagnostics, repair, and maintenance under the watchful eyes of seasoned aviation engineers. The aircraft hangar and workshops were there learning fields. The deafening roar of jet engines became a familiar soundtrack as they delved into the complexities of naval aviation machinery.

The training extended beyond the hangers and workshops. Varun and his fellow trainees were introduced to the flight deck environment, gaining firsthand experience in the fast-paced world of aircraft machine operations. They observed and learnt the seamless choreography of take-offs and landings on the deck of aircraft carriers, an integral aspect of naval aviation, while on their training visit to the mighty Aircraft carriers and on other frontline ships to learn about helicopter operations. Simulators became the trainees' virtual playgrounds, allowing them to practice and refine their skills in a controlled environment. Varun found himself behind the controls of a virtual aircraft, learning through various scenarios that mimicked real-world challenges. It was a crucial aspect of their training, preparing them for the dynamic and unpredictable nature of naval aviation.

Throughout the two-year training at Garuda, Varun and his peers, developed a profound appreciation for the synergy in the context of naval aviation. They worked as a cohesive unit with mechanical aviation engineers, understanding that the success of a mission depended on their collective expertise and efficiency. As they neared the end of their training, Varun felt a sense of accomplishment and readiness. The vast skies awaited them, and they were well-prepared to contribute to the naval aviation wing of the Indian Navy. The friendships forged during their time at Garuda mirrored the bonds formed in earlier training establishments – strong, resilient, and ready to support each other in the soaring challenges that lay ahead.

As Varun gazed at the naval aircrafts and helicopters on the runway at Cochin airport, he knew that the journey was far from over. The wings of naval artificers were not just mechanical and electrical; they were the wings of aspirations, dreams, and a commitment to serving their nation with distinction in the realm of naval aviation. Another story of an Electrical Aviation Artificer was now in the making.

End of an Exciting Journey

As the sun dipped below the horizon, casting a warm glow over the naval training base in Visakhapatnam, Vishal, Arjun, Pradeep, Jagdeesh, Ravinder and Rajat, all stood on the threshold of a new chapter in their lives. After four rigorous years of training, they were finally ready to embark on their careers in the Indian Navy as a trained Shipwright Artificer Engineer.

With excitement coursing through their veins, Vishal and his comrades eagerly awaited their posting assignments. They knew that they would soon be serving on naval ships and shipyards, putting their training to use in the service of their country. But what filled them with even greater anticipation was the prospect of working alongside their counterparts from other naval training institutes. Marine engineers from INS Shivaji, electrical engineers from INS Valsura, and aviation engineers from INS Garuda—they would all come together as Partner to form a cohesive unit, each bringing their own expertise to the table.

As they waited for their posting assignments to be announced, Vishal and others exchanged stories and shared their hopes and aspirations for the future. They knew that the strong bonds forged during their training would only grow stronger as they faced the challenges and adventures that lay ahead. Finally, the moment arrived. Assignments were posted, and Vishal's heart swelled with pride as he read his name alongside the designation of a shipwright artificer fifth engineer on board INS Amba, a submarine support ship while Jagdeesh and Ravinder were posted on India's only aircraft carrier, INS Vikrant. All his fellow friends received their own postings on naval ships, each filled with excitement for the opportunities that awaited them.

They all prepared to set sail on their respective journeys, Vishal and others knew that they were part of something greater than themselves. Together, they would serve their country with dedication and honour, upholding the proud traditions of the Indian Navy and forging bonds that would last a lifetime.

PART 2

NAVAL JOURNEY

Harmony of Steel and Sea

The salt-laden breeze welcomed Vishal as he stepped onto the deck of the massive naval ship, a specialised submarine depot ship berthed at Naval Dockyard (Bombay), just behind aircraft carrier INS Vikrant, he would call home for the next few years. Fresh out of naval engineering training, Vishal's eyes widened as he looked at the imposing structure that would be his workplace, a marvel of steel and technology that danced with the rhythm of the sea.

Assigned as a shipwright artificer fifth engineer as his first practical ground, Vishal quickly became acquainted with the inner workings of the ship. His duties ranged from assisting for planned preventive maintenance of ship, hull surveys, deck machinery maintenance, monitoring ship's hull potential, learning about troubleshooting of defects and glitches in the machinery. The noise of the running machineries and ventilation fans, the creaking of the ship, and the distant roar of the ocean created a symphony that echoed through the vessel.

As he navigated the labyrinth of corridors below deck, Vishal found himself in awe of the intricate systems that powered the ship. His mentor, Chief Artificer Nair and Joshua, became a guiding figure, imparting wisdom acquired through years at sea. With a weathered face and eyes that held the knowledge of countless voyages, shipwright officer Naidu instilled in Vishal the importance of teamwork, discipline, and adaptability.

Days at sea were a cascade of challenges and triumphs. Vishal observed and learned to troubleshoot while working with his seniors. Sometime watching his other counterpart from engine rooms and electrical engineer gave immense knowledge of working with malfunctioning system on board. The ship became more than a vessel; it became a living entity, each component working in harmony to defy the elements. Amidst the challenges, camaraderie thrived among the fellow artificers, and became a second family. Late-night working inside machinery compartments or the open decks turned into shared stories of far-off shores, dreams, and the love of the open sea. The mess hall buzzed with laughter as the crew swapped tales of their adventures.

One day, as the ship sailed through calm waters under a brilliant sunset, Vishal found himself on the upper deck, gazing out at the vast expanse of the ocean. The rhythmic rise and fall of the waves mirrored the ebb and flow of his journey. He marvelled at the realization that the vastness of the sea was a reflection of the boundless possibilities that lay ahead in his career.

As the months passed, Vishal's confidence and skills grew. He became adept at anticipating the ship's needs, ensuring its systems ran like a well-oiled machine. Whether it was conducting routine inspections or responding to unexpected challenges, Vishal embraced each task with the same determination that had fuelled his journey from the naval engineering institute to the vast deck of the ship. His time on the naval ship became a chapter in a story of growth, resilience, and the indomitable spirit of exploration. And as the ship continued its journey through the endless horizon, Vishal, a fresh-faced engineer, stood on its deck, ready to face the unknown challenges that lay ahead, his heart beating in rhythm with the pulse of the sea.

An Electrical Engineer's Odessey

While Vishal moved to Bombay to serve onboard INS Amba, Vishal's peer Ashok Kaushal, a bright-eyed electrical artificer trainee embarked on his journey from INS Valsura, eager to learn and serve his country in the esteemed Indian Navy. Hailing from Delhi, he had always harboured a deep sense and desire to contribute to the defence of his nation. It was at Valsura, among the whirring machinery and bustling corridors, that Ashok found his true calling as electrical artificer.

As a C-stream based electrical artificer, Ashok a control expert dedicated himself wholeheartedly to his training, immersing himself in the intricacies of naval electrical systems and technologies. For four years, he honed his skills at INS Valsura, soaking up knowledge and experience like a sponge. When the time came to embark on the next chapter of his naval career, Ashok was filled with a mixture of excitement and trepidation. He bid farewell to his friends and mentors at INS Valsura and boarded the Russian origin Indian Naval Ship Kavaratti, bound for the port city of Vishakhapatnam.

As Kavaratti sailed through the azure waters of the Indian Ocean and Bay of Bengal, Ashok felt a surge of pride and anticipation course through his veins. He was ready to begin his service life, to contribute his skills and expertise to the defence of his nation. Over the next fifteen years, Ashok's career will take him on a remarkable journey of growth and transformation. Starting out on the Petya class Kavaratti, he learned the ropes of shipboard life, mastering the intricacies of electrical systems and machinery.

But Ashok's thirst for knowledge and adventure knew no bounds, and he soon found himself transferred to a larger, more advanced SNF class Destroyer INS Rajput, a Russian origin ship, laced with both air and long-range guided surface missiles. Here, he faced new challenges and opportunities, navigating the complexities of modern naval warfare with skill and determination. With each passing year, Ashok's confidence and expertise grew, earning him the respect of his peers and superiors alike. But despite his success, he never forgot his roots or the lessons he had learned at INS Valsura.

When the time came for Ashok to move on from sea service, he knew exactly where he wanted to go. Returning to his alma mater as a trainee instructor at INS Valsura, he found himself once again surrounded by fond memories. As Ashok passed on his knowledge and experience to the next generation of naval trainees, he couldn't help but feel a sense of pride and satisfaction. He had come full circle, from wide-eyed recruit to seasoned instructor, and his journey was far from over.

A Move- Change of Base Port

Vishal was living his dream at the Indian Naval Ship Amba. Slowly he gained confidence of his superior and was frequently called out to assist. As he completed a year into the job, he was promoted next to Shipwright Artificer 4th engineer. INS Amba, stationed at the bustling port of Bombay, was not only a vessel of immense power but also a tight-knit community.

One fine morning, as Vishal was inspecting the ship's hull for routine maintenance, he overheard a buzz among the crew. The news spread like wildfire – INS Amba was about to change its command, and the base port would shift from Bombay to Vizag for its long refit. The announcement of command change caught many by surprise, including Vishal. As the news sank in, the crew members, both unmarried and those with families, found themselves grappling with mixed emotions. The prospect of leaving the familiar surroundings of Bombay, where many had their roots, was met with a range of reactions. Some were excited about the change, seeing it as an opportunity for new adventures and experiences. Others, especially those with families, were concerned about uprooting their lives and settling in a new city.

As the day of departure approached, the crew prepared INS Amba for the journey ahead. The ship set sail from Bombay, leaving behind the iconic cityscape, and made its enroute port calls at Goa and Cochin. The crew, despite their initial apprehensions, found comfort in the routine of naval life. Vishal, too, adapted quickly, forging bonds with his fellow sailors. The ship's itinerary included a port visit to Trincomalee, a serene coastal city in Sri Lanka on eastern coast. From Cochin, INS Amba charted a course to Trincomalee in Sri Lanka. The crew embraced the unique experience of exploring foreign ports and interacting with local cultures. The ship became a floating home, and the crew became a family, supporting each other through the challenges of naval life. The crew, always ready for a break from naval routines, looked forward to exploring new cuisines, and perhaps doing a bit of shopping. When INS Amba docked in Trincomalee, the crew, including Vishal, disembarked with a sense of curiosity. The city, with its historical significance and picturesque landscapes, provided the perfect backdrop for their exploration. The atmosphere was peaceful, and the island seemed untouched by the political turmoil that would later affect the region.

Vishal, as well as his friends with a keen interest in the local craftsmanship, decided to venture into the markets of Trincomalee. The bustling bazaars were filled with vibrant fabrics, Electronics, and other foreign goods, hard to find in India those days, and unique artifacts. He admired the craftsmanship of the local artisans, eager to bring back souvenirs that would remind him of this exotic locale. The crew was particularly eager to shop electronics and clothes as these came cheaper being duty free. Aside from shopping, the crew took the opportunity to explore the historical sites in Trincomalee. They visited ancient temples, explored the colonial-era architecture, and even enjoyed the pristine beaches that the city had to offer. The camaraderie among the sailors grew stronger as they shared these memorable experiences.

As INS Amba prepared to leave Trincomalee, the crew boarded the ship with a sense of fulfilment. Vishal, with his bag full of Japanese tape recorder, watch, camera, and unique souvenirs, reflected on the unexpected joy of exploring a peaceful island in the midst of a naval journey. Little did they know that the tranquillity of Trincomalee would become a poignant memory, as the island would face challenging times in the years to come. But on that sunny day in early 1983, the crew of INS Amba sailed away, grateful for the peaceful interlude in a foreign port, carrying the warmth of Sri Lanka with them as they continued their naval journey.

Finally, as the ship approached Vizag, the crew's anticipation grew. The sight of the city's coastline and the protected harbour of naval dockyard welcomed them to their new home. The crew, once hesitant about the change, now looked forward to creating new memories in Vizag. The transition from Bombay to Vizag had not only strengthened the crew's bond but had also moulded Vishal into an integral part of INS Amba's legacy. As the ship finally berthed at Vizag, after long sailing for its long refit, the crew looked forward with a sense of accomplishment to upcoming development. Vishal was particularly happy to unite with Ashok there, who was serving on INS Kavaratti at Visakhapatnam.

It's Not all Work- But Sports Too

Vishal was immersed not only in his responsibilities on the ship but also the passion for cricket that ran through his veins since his school days and later during training days in Bombay and Vishakhapatnam. After having played for ship's cricket team, he was now representing Eastern Naval Command team for command championship. Vishal's talent as an all-rounder cricketer didn't go unnoticed during the command tournament. His impressive performances with both bat and ball caught the eye of selectors, and he was elated to receive the news that he had been chosen to represent the navy team in the upcoming inter-services tournament. All selected players for navy team remained to at Vishakhapatnam to practice for services tournament, to be held at Delhi few weeks later.

The prospect of playing in a tournament that brings together the best cricketers from the Army, Navy, and Air Force filled Vishal with excitement. The tournament was not just an opportunity for friendly rivalry but also a platform where exceptional players could catch the eye of selector and potentially play for services team in the Ranji Trophy. However, fate had a different plan for Vishal. A few days before the crucial inter services cricket tournament, disaster struck during a routine practice session in the ground of INS Satvahana. Vishal, known for his good batting and disciplined bowling, suffered a severe blow as he broke his left arm while attempting a catch at slips during practice session. The disappointment hung in the air. Vishal, who had worked hard to earn his spot in the navy team, now faced the harsh reality of missing the tournament due to the unfortunate injury. As Vishal nursed his injury and watched from the sideline, his teammates prepared for the tournament, he couldn't help but feel a sense of disappointment and frustration. He had worked so hard to earn his spot on the team, only to have his dreams shattered by a single moment of misfortune.

Despite the setback, Vishal remained resilient. He focused on his recovery, undergoing intensive rehabilitation to heal his arm as quickly as possible. He continued to support his team from the sideline, offering words of encouragement during practice. Later, Navy team played valiantly, but Vishal couldn't help but wonder what if he had been out there on the field with his teammates. And while his cricketing career may have been put on hold, his dedication and determination never wavered.

The missed opportunity to play in the services tournament left a lingering sense of what-ifs for Vishal. The Ranji Trophy, the pinnacle of domestic cricket in India, seemed like a distant dream that had slipped through his fingers. However, Vishal's resilience and commitment to both his naval duties and his love for cricket remained unwavering.

As INS Amba was fast getting ready to sail through the waters after its long refit and dry docking, Vishal continued to contribute his skills and expertise to the naval operations. Though his cricketing aspirations had taken a hit, his time on the ship had instilled in him a sense of discipline and teamwork that would serve him well in both his naval career and beyond.

Harbor of Challenges: The Naval Engineer's Odyssey

Vishal, by mid of 1983 received his posting orders to another ship at Vizag and as he stood on the dock, staring at the naval vessel known as Landing Ship, Tank (LST) named INS Ghorpad that would be his workplace and home for the next deployments. After near two years of service on a submarine support ship, he was ready for a new challenge. He was joining to replace his senior Prakash Yadav, who would be taking up another assignment shortly. The naval landing ship, designed for amphibious operations, would test his engineering skills in unfamiliar waters.

The LST, a highly specialized design that enables ocean sailing and shore grounding. With its flat keel that allows it to be beached and stay upright. Its propellers and rudder have guarded protection from grounding. With an optimised hull form and propulsion LST vessels are characterised by excellent seakeeping and a very efficient logistics arrangement for embarked forces. Complying with the latest stability requirements, the LST offers a high degree of survivability because of its extra strong double hull. The ships are designed with an innovative ballast system which allowed the flat-bottomed ships to increase its draft during ocean transit for seaworthiness purposes, and pumping out the ballast tanks dry, allows it to raise up in the water, facilitating shallow-draft landing operations.

As Vishal boarded the vessel, he felt a surge of excitement mixed with a tinge of uncertainty. The ship's steel frame seemed to echo with the history of past missions and the challenges that lay ahead. He made his way to the ship's machinery compartments, where the sound of machinery greeted him like an old friend. Prakash briefed Vishal all about the ship and area which will require his special attention now onward. The first few days aboard the naval landing craft were a whirlwind of activities. Vishal familiarized himself with the ship's unique systems – deck machineries optimized for beach landings, winches and capstan, specialized cargo bays, bow doors, ramps, and the intricate hydraulics that would facilitate amphibious operations. His expertise from the last ship was invaluable, but he knew he had much to learn in this new environment. The crew, a tight-knit group of sailors including some senior to him, welcomed Vishal with open arms. They recognized his experience and eagerness to contribute to the mission. The naval landing ship was tasked with transporting marines and equipment to remote shores, a critical aspect of naval operations.

As the ship set sail for his first mission, Vishal found himself engrossed in the operational intricacies of amphibious landings. Prakash was still there to guide him through his first operational mission. He worked closely with executive officer Lieutenant Commander Arvind and others, ensuring the ship's beaching, mooring, and anchoring machineries were all in perfect shape for a successful mission of landing and beaching operations. The roar of distant thud of heavy equipment being moved on the deck and cargo area became the soundtrack of his days. During challenging mission, sometimes the seas were rough, and the landing zone was far from ideal. Vishal watched his fellow shipmate, engineers working tirelessly under challenging conditions. The crew faced a series of unexpected obstacles, from unpredictable weather to unforeseen equipment malfunctions. Through it all, engineering prowess of technical teams and leadership shone, earning respect of the crew.

Life aboard the landing ship was a constant ebb and flow of challenges and victories. Vishal along with his team conducted routine maintenance between missions, addressing the wear and tear from the harsh maritime environment. He was awed by efficiency of the crew, each member playing a crucial role in the seamless operation of the vessel. As the deployment progressed, Vishal's appreciation for the landing ship deepened. The ship, once a foreign entity, became an extension of himself. He revelled in the dynamic nature of amphibious operations, the unpredictable nature of beach landings, and the satisfaction of overcoming engineering hurdles at sea.

Lord Varuna and Chants of Har-Har Mahadev

It was during a beaching mission with Army troops near Kakinada that Vishal's skills as a naval artificer engineer were truly put to the test. A sudden storm swept in from the horizon, battering the landing craft with powerful winds and towering waves. As the vessel pitched and rolled in the turbulent waters, Vishal sprang into action, rallying his team to ensure the ship's systems remained secured and operational.

Earlier, the day was drenched in excitement as the renowned Mahar regiment of Indian Army eagerly boarded the INS Ghorpad for a beaching exercise, ready to showcase their prowess alongside tanks and artillery. As the ship departed Vishakhapatnam harbour, the troops, lined up and standing on both sides of deck, brimming with enthusiasm, chanted "Har- Har Mahadev" with infectious josh, filled the air with their spirited camaraderie. Decked in full military regalia, the troops felt invincible, proud to be part of a mission that would undoubtedly leave an indelible mark. The tanks, artillery, and soldiers were all in high spirits, ready to face the challenge of beaching with unwavering enthusiasm.

However, as INS Ghorpad left harbour and entered the open sea, the troops soon found themselves in uncharted waters—both literally and metaphorically. The once euphoric army soldiers began to feel the unexpected effects of the high sea waves and the ship's rolling and pitching motion. As the ship encountered open sea, the waves played a whimsical game, tossing the vessel with gleeful abandon. The troops, who had been riding the waves of enthusiasm just moments ago, suddenly found themselves incapacitated. The Har-Har Mahadev chants transformed into gasps for fresh air, and the josh was replaced by groans of discomfort. The sea, it seemed, had other plans for the proud soldiers of the Mahar regiment. The rolling and pitching motion of the ship, a foreign experience to many, turned the once spirited troops into a sea of wobbling soldiers, holding on to anything sturdy for dear life.

Laughter echoed across the ship among sailors as soldiers succumbed to the inevitable reality of sea sickness. The once pristine decks became an impromptu battlefield of vomit, with soldiers lying sprawled in various states of discomfort. Even the tanks and artillery, stoic in their metal frames, couldn't escape the effects of the unpredictable sea. It was a sight to behold—the fearless soldiers of the Mahar regiment, now rendered temporarily incapacitated by the relentless sea. In the midst of the chaos, a wry smile crossed Vishal's face. The unpredictable nature of the sea had played its part in humbling even the most spirited troops. It was a lesson learned in the most unexpected of classrooms—the open sea.

As the ship continued its journey, the once boisterous soldiers slowly acclimated to the relentless rocking of the vessel. The waves that had initially seemed insurmountable became a testament to the adaptability and resilience of the Mahar regiment. Vishal could feel the admiration in soldier's eye for their naval counterpart. And so, amidst the laughter, groans, and occasional chants of "Har-Har Mahadev," the INS Ghorpad sailed forward, leaving behind a sea of memories that would be shared with chuckles and camaraderie for years to come.

Mission – Beaching on the Shore

As INS Ghorpad, a formidable LST, sailed through the Bay of Bengal with a critical mission at hand, its shipwright artificer engineer, Vishal faced an unprecedented challenge as the bow door, essential for offloading army troops and tanks, refused to budge. The hydraulic system, vital for the smooth functioning of the door, had malfunctioned, leaving Vishal with a race against time. The urgency of the situation was evident. The Mahar regiment troops and their tanks, vital for the mission, were stranded onboard, ready to disembark at Kakinada. Every passing moment increased the stakes, and Vishal knew that exceptional effort was required to overcome this mechanical setback. Vishal along with support team embarked on an intensive diagnostic process to identify the root cause of the malfunction. They were deeply engaged checking system drawings and manual. The clock was ticking, and the pressure was palpable. The very success of the mission hinged on the timely offloading of the troops and tanks. Failure was not an option.

Undeterred by the complexity of the hydraulic failure, Vishal exhibited remarkable leadership, rallying his technical team to work relentlessly. They checked for oil leakages in the system and eventually dismantled the hydraulic piping system, meticulously examining each component for signs of damage. Vishal's experience in ship's engineering became the beacon guiding the team through the intricate web of the malfunction. As the sun dipped below the horizon, Vishal and his team worked under the harsh glare of flood lights. The sound of tools clinking against metal echoed through the vast expanse of the ship and cargo hold. The pressure was immense, but Vishal's unwavering determination fuelled the team's collective effort.

The Mahar regiment troops, aware of the situation, maintained a stoic resolve. The tanks, formidable machines of war, stood silent in the ship's belly, witnesses to the herculean effort taking place around them. The Commanding Officer and other crew of INS Ghorpad, driven by a commitment to the mission, pressed on, fully aware that the stakes were higher than ever. After hours of tireless work, Vishal pinpointed the issue—a critical hydraulic hose had burst and a three-way valve in the hydraulic system had seized. The team mobilized quickly to rectify the problem, replacing the malfunctioning valve held as onboard spare for just such emergencies. Luckily, the leaking hydraulic hose coupling was close to the tank head above the water level. The gravity of problem was severe since bow and ramp door became non-operational. But with sheer hard work and commitment, team replaced the hose while working inside the tank, neck deep into the water with only head outside. Thankfully, they ensured and prevented contamination in the hydraulic system from ingress of sea water. As Vishal activated the hydraulic control system once again, there was a moment of suspense before the bow door slowly began to creak open and ramp started lower down. The sense of relief was palpable, but there was no time for celebration. The troops and tanks needed to be offloaded swiftly to meet the mission's timeline.

Captain carefully watched all around the ship while executive officer took situation report from each post and started giving instructions over handsets. Ship started to move slowly for its beaching attempt under controlled engine power, aft winch releasing steel wires under control, one end of wires connected to the aft anchor dropped about quarter mile away while approaching the beach. With careful steering ship moved forward, navigation team on bridge keenly eyeing sea depth on echo sounder, suddenly forward hull bottom touched sand with a thud, pushing and pressing the sand underneath for some distance and finally rested on the soft beach land, aft body of ship still floating, engine roaring for any emergency situation, Captain instructed all posts to keep a watch while all prepared to offload the military men and cargo.

Most army soldiers by now had recovered from the horror faced on their departure from Vishakhapatnam port and have survived on Khichadi and Rasam during entire sailing. With a military precision, the Mahar regiment troops disembarked, their boots hitting the deck with purpose with bag packs on, few men with communication sets on their back, others holding rifles overhead with both their hands raised up. While disembarking they traversed the sea water waist deep in water, some fearing from drowning but moved forward struggling, and one by one all crossed to the shore. Tanks rolled off the ship, floating for a while propelled by their wheel chain belts until touched the land, ready for deployment. As the sun rose over Kakinada, the Mahar regiment troops and their tanks were on shore for military exercise, ready to execute their assigned mission.

Vishal, a shipwright engineer, stood on ship's deck, his gaze fixed on the horizon. The challenges faced and overcome were a testament to the indomitable spirit and expertise of the Indian Navy, ensuring that the nation's defence remained unyielding in the face of adversity. The commanding officer and the executive officer had a sigh of relief writ on their faces. Their grim faces turned into a mild smile. Colonel in charge of landing troop was all praise for the team's effort under high pressure environment. Vishal watched with a mix of pride and satisfaction as the mission unfolded successfully, his exceptional effort ensuring that the ship fulfilled its critical role in completing the mission.

Once the bow doors and ramp closed fully, now was the time to shift the action to ship's rear for beached ship to float back fully and move into sea. They will have to come back again to recover the troops and tanks next day. Ships large aft wire winches came into action as ship started to drift back with engine power on assisted by pull of steel wires, while anchor securely dug into the seabed. Once ship reached closer to anchor and recovered it fully, ship pulled full ahead and sailed towards the deep sea. Next morning, while it was still dark, ship made another beaching action to recover the troops and tanks and sailed back into deep sea for a return voyage to their base port Vishakhapatnam.

Upon returning to port after a successful deployment, standing on the deck, Vishal looked at the naval landing craft with a sense of pride. The ship had weathered the challenges of the mission, and so had he. As he disembarked, Vishal knew that his experience aboard the naval landing ship had not only expanded his engineering expertise but also forged a bond with a unique vessel and a crew that had become a second family. Ready for the next deployment, he carried the lessons of the open seas and the challenges of amphibious operations with him, a seasoned naval engineer with a harbour of experiences in his wake.

As one and half years passed by, he learnt of his next posting to a newly commissioned frigate, first indigenously designed and built ship in India INS Godavari. He was happy to be back to Bombay once again where the ship had its base port.

Life on a Newly Commissioned Ship

In the early 1980s, as Indian Navy prepared to commission its first fully indigenously designed and constructed guided missile frigate, INS Godavari, Rameshwar, a seasoned Shipwright Artificer, Third Engineer, found himself at the heart of this historic venture. Stationed at Mazagaon Dock Ltd., he was assigned as part of the commissioning crew responsible for ship's take over from shipyard. His responsibility was ensuring the ship's hull, structural components, and machinery met the rigorous standards set by the Navy in the specifications.

Godavari was an upgraded version of Nilgiris class of frigates of European design. It was 126-meter-long ship with beam of 14.5 m and full displacement of 3800 tons. It was propelled by two steam turbines generating 22400 kw for full speed of 28 knots. It carried four surface to surface missiles (SSM) and twenty-four surface to air missiles (SAM) in its armour in addition rocket launchers and heavy guns.

As the ship took shape under the skilled hands of the shipbuilder, Rameshwar oversaw every aspect of its hull construction part. His keen eye for detail and unwavering commitment to excellence earned him the respect of both his fellow crew members and the shipyard personnel. While he was working on structural aspects, his counterpart's engine room artificers and electrical and aviation artificers dabbled in their area of responsibilities. Their expertise played a crucial role in ensuring INS Godavari met the stringent standards required for naval service. Post-commissioning of ship, Rameshwar continued his service on board INS Godavari as crew.

Fate took an unexpected turn during one stormy day at sea while leaving harbour. Rameshwar, driven by his unwavering dedication, was working on the anchor capstan, when ship's forecastle suddenly dived deep into sea as a massive wave struck the ship with force. In the tumultuous conditions, he and few other were swept away by the wave just short of falling overboard, leaving his fellow crew members in shock and disbelief. The incident rendered Rameshwar with broken knee and medically unfit for service on board the ship. As he faced a challenging road to recovery, the navy looked to find a replacement for his role. Enters Vishal, an eighteen-months-junior Shipwright Artificer, and a fellow Delhiite and cricket teammate. Vishal, a friend and admirer of Rameshwar's resilience and dedication, stepped into his shoes to continue the important work. Vishal now was to work under his senior Master Chief Shipwright Artificer Pushkar on the ship.

Vishal, an engineer, and ship constructor by training, harboured a dream that went beyond the conventional bounds of his profession – to serve on a frontline warship, a frigate, a vessel that would be the pride of India for many years to come. This ship stood as a symbol of both tradition and innovation, a beacon of pride for the nation. Armed with the training and camaraderie forged during their naval artificer days, Vishal seamlessly assumed Rameshwar's responsibilities. The baton was passed from one Delhiite to another, both united by their love for the sea, their commitment to the Navy, and their shared admiration for Amitabh Bachchan.

Though the circumstances were bittersweet, Rameshwar's legacy lived on through Vishal, who carried forward the dedication and commitment to excellence instilled by his predecessor. As INS Godavari continued its service to the nation, the spirit of resilience, camaraderie, and duty echoed in the halls of the ship, a testament to the indomitable spirit of naval artificers like Rameshwar and Vishal.

Seafarer's Ingenuity: Riding the Waves

With unwavering determination, Vishal set out to make his dream a reality. He toiled tirelessly on-board ship Godavari, learning from his seniors, collaborating with skilled craftsmen and engineers. His vision was clear – to learn everything on frigate built with modern technology with Indian craftsmanship, a floating testament to the nation's maritime prowess. Ship donned many advanced weapon systems, carried two helicopters with landing deck and stowage hangers. As Vishal set sail on the Godavari for its maiden voyage, he felt a surge of emotion. The sea beneath him seemed to echo the pulse of the nation, and the sails billowed with the hopes and aspirations of those who had contributed to the frigate's creation.

Vishal's journey with the Godavari had just begun, fresh from his last assignment on a Landing Ship. From the engine rooms to other machinery compartments from lowest to the topmost deck, he quickly apprised himself about the ships topology armed with ships General Arrangement drawings to other ship system plans, every inch of the ship was soon back of his hand. His expertise lay in hull and machinery maintenance, a role he embraced with passion and dedication. The Godavari, with its sleek design and cutting-edge technology, was a symbol of India's naval prowess. Vishal's responsibilities included ensuring that every piece of machinery he was responsible to look after, hummed with precision and that the ship's hull and associated machineries remained impervious to the relentless embrace of the sea.

The Vishal's voyages weren't confined to the Indian shores. Captain Rustamji, along with his dedicated crew, undertook missions across the vast expanse of the Indian Ocean and ventured into international waters. The missile frigate became a familiar sight, gliding majestically into seas around the world, representing India's maritime prowess. The missions were as diverse as the sea itself. From conducting war exercises to patrolling of seas to humanitarian aid missions, the Vishal noted how its crew faced every challenge with grace and ingenuity. Captain Rustamji, with his unique blend of expertise and a keen understanding of the sea, ably supported by his executive officer Commander Arun Bisht earned accolades not only for the frigate's operation but also for its impeccable performance. But beyond the accolades, Captain Rustamji always remained grounded, driven by a deep love for the sea and the nation he served. And so, as the sun dipped below the horizon, casting hues of orange and gold over the Godavari's decks, Captain Rustamji looked out at the vast expanse of the sea. The frigate cut through the waves, carrying with it the legacy of innovation and the spirit of a seafarer who dared to dream, design, and sail into uncharted waters.

During 1985, The then prime minister of India Shri Rajiv Gandhi and minster of state for defence Shri Arun Singh boarded the vessel. They were accompanied by Navy Chief Admiral RH Tahiliani for two days to witness the naval exercise at sea. They keenly watched different naval operations from wheelhouse and fire control room, and those working behind the action. They took time out and went around to see important part of the ship as per a planned route. Next day morning prime minister had breakfast with crew in the mess and mingled freely with them.

Life at Sea- A Stormy Affaire

On a moonlit night in the vast expanse of the open sea, the naval ship, INS Godavari, sailed through calm waters with a dedicated crew on board. The ship was on a mission, and the crew, comprising sailors from various departments, went about their duties with discipline and dedication. As the ship ventured further into the sea, the weather took an unexpected turn. Dark clouds gathered on the horizon, and the wind began to howl, signalling the onset of an approaching storm. The once tranquil sea transformed into a tumultuous expanse of rolling waves. The executive officer, quickly made the necessary preparations, securing loose items on the ship and instructing the crew to brace for the storm. The sailors, accustomed to facing the unpredictable nature of the sea, took their positions with a sense of resilience and determination.

As the storm hit with full force, the ship was tossed and turned by the powerful waves. The violent roll and pitch of the vessel made even the most seasoned sailors feel the queasy onset of seasickness. Yet, duty called, and the crew pushed through their discomfort to ensure the ship's safety and continued operation.

In the engine room department, Master Chief Artificer Kumar and his team battled against the relentless motion of the ship to keep the engines and other machineries running. Despite the relentless sway, they were on toes to maintain the ship's propulsion and allied machineries, ensuring it could navigate through the storm.

Down in the galley and dining hall, the ship's cooks faced a unique challenge. The heavy roll and pitch made it impossible to operate the dining mess. The clatter of trays, dishes, and cutlery echoed through the metal walls as the crew members attempted to secure their meals. Recognizing the futility of dining in such conditions, the galley crew quickly shifted to serving lightweight and easily portable meals to crew members on duty. Rice and Rasam was the most preferred meal under these circumstances, but many who felt seasick went without food. The corridors and washrooms in ship resembled pool of vomit. Wheelhouse was no better, but crew was still on vigil. Those off duty just rested on beds under the horrific situation.

Despite the challenging conditions, the crew displayed remarkable resilience. They adapted to the constant motion of the ship, continuing their duties with a sense of commitment. Each department worked cohesively, supporting one another through the turbulent night. As the storm eventually subsided, the sea gradually returned to its calm state. The crew, tired and worn, took a moment to catch their breath. They had weathered the storm together, showcasing the unwavering spirit that defined life on a naval ship.

Flying Machine-Trapped in a Cage

The operational sailing mission of INS Godavari was proceeding smoothly, with naval vessel cutting through the waves with precision. One day, ship's Sea King helicopter, a crucial asset for the mission, was scheduled for a sortie. However, fate had other plans.

As the crew prepared for the helicopter's deployment, an unexpected challenge emerged. The helicopter hangar door, refused to budge. Vishal, heard his name on main broadcast and reached ship's hanger, quickly assessed the situation, and discovered that the roller shutter mechanism had suffered an electro-mechanical failure. The shaft connected to motor, responsible for raising the roller shutter was not rotating, rendering the entire system non-operational. The urgency of the situation was apparent. As an emergency, the shutter door was tried with manual mode, but it failed. Without the helicopter, the mission's capabilities would be severely compromised. Vishal, driven by a sense of duty and determination, knew he had to act swiftly to find a solution.

With encouragement from his Executive Officer, Commander Bisht, Vishal formulated a daring plan to restore the roller shutter system to working order. The inspection cover of the motor housing was on hanger top at ship side end. It was a high-risk endeavour that involved working on the top edge of the ship's hanger, while the vessel was still in sailing mode. One wrong move could spell disaster. Undeterred by the daunting task ahead, Vishal and his team sprang into action. They meticulously assessed the damage and devised a plan to repair the roller shutter door. Armed with determination and a sense of duty, they set to work, harness tied around, braving the elements and the unpredictable movements of the ship. All rallied behind Vishal, helping to support whatever needed. Their collective determination fuelled their efforts, driving them to overcome every obstacle in their path.

As the hours passed, Vishal's technical skills shone through. With steady hands and unwavering focus, he worked tirelessly to disconnect the damaged motor shaft and gear assembly, ensuring that each component was secured with precision and care. Fortunately, the shaft was intact, but a connecting cotter pin of coupling had sheared. The replacement part was not in the spares inventory. A new cotter pin was manufactured temporarily to the size in workshop and replaced, which eventually worked and made the shaft rotate once again. Finally, after hours of relentless effort and teamwork, team achieved success. The roller shutter made operational once again, releasing the trapped Sea King helicopter.

Cheers erupted on ship's helicopter deck as the crew celebrated victory over adversity.

As the INS Godavari continued its operational mission, technical team's effort and courage served as a testament to the unwavering commitment, no matter how daunting. And as they sailed into the horizon, they did so with the knowledge that they were prepared for whatever lay ahead, united in their resolve to defend and protect their nation's interests at sea.

A Dreadful Night

It was a peaceful late evening aboard the INS Godavari as the on-duty crew went about their duties, the gentle hum of the ship's machineries and sound of ventilation fans provided backdrop to the night. Ship had returned just two days back from weeklong exercise mission at sea. Nonduty crew had either gone home or were out ashore for outing in the city. Little did they know, however, that a single moment of carelessness would soon plunge them into a race against time.

As the clock struck midnight, some off duty crew members returning to the ship after drink and dining, tempered with switches mounted on the side bulkheads, probably by mischief as they entered the ship from main door. Suddenly, the sprinkler and flooding system inside the Surface to Air Missile (SAM) housing chamber got activated. In an instant, water began to cascade down into the missile chamber, flooding the chamber and soaking everything in its path. The water under pressure got sprayed into the loaded missiles. Once water started to overflow, lobby around the chamber also got flooded ultimately water leading to the cabin's areas.

Panic ensued as the alarm rang out throughout the ship, alerting the crew to the emergency unfolding below deck. The Chief of Weapon Systems, duty electrical engineer, the shipwright engineer, and the duty watch crew sprang into action, their training kicking in as they rushed to contain the flooding and assess the damage. The electrical supply for the entire system was checked and ensured that it's cut off. With the missiles submerged in water, there was no time to waste. The technical team worked tirelessly throughout the night, braving the spray of water as they pumped out the flooded chamber and cleaned the contaminated surface of the missiles and chamber.

Meanwhile, the duty officer of the day kept the Commanding Officer briefed of the situation, ensuring that they were kept informed of the progress being made to salvage the situation. Executive officer and senior electrical officer too joined in the salvage action to guide the operation. Despite the late hour and the daunting task at hand, the crew worked together seamlessly, their determination unwavering as they battled against the odds to restore safety and order to the ship. As the first light of dawn broke over the horizon, the technical team finally emerged from the missile chamber, exhausted but victorious. Through their unwavering dedication and teamwork, they managed to salvage the situation, preventing any further damage to the ship or its valuable cargo.

As the crew gathered for their morning briefing, the Commanding Officer commended the efforts of the team, praising their quick thinking and decisive action in the face of adversity. It was a reminder of the importance of remaining vigilant, even in moments of relaxation, and of the remarkable resilience of the human spirit in times of crisis. The special weapon expert team of Naval Dockyard arrived for the checks and rectification and went through their SOP. The salvage and repair of a SAM chamber with a missile loaded inside, contaminated due to accidental flooding, is a complex and meticulous process that requires the expertise of skilled technicians and engineers.

An emergency response action was initiated immediately to isolate the affected area.

Crew was notified through main broadcast about the emergency to ensure everyone is aware and can respond accordingly.

Safety zones was established and for controlled access to the contaminated chamber.

Assessment of Contamination was done to evaluate the extent of water damage and contamination on the missile, launch chamber, and associated systems.

Water salinity was checked to determine the level of damage.

Missiles and Chamber were carefully inspected for any external and internal damage caused by water exposure.

Specialized dehumidifiers and fans were used to remove moisture from the launch chamber.

Electronics and Guidance System was Inspected and examined for signs of damage or malfunction.

Rigorous quality assurance checks were conducted on both the missile and launch chamber to verify their operational status. Perform functional tests and simulations to ensure the missile's readiness for future deployment. The entire process required a coordinated effort from various departments and specialized personnel, emphasizing safety, precision, and adherence to established protocols throughout the entire salvage and repair operation. Electrical officer, Electrical Artificers and other weapon crew remained ever cautious for many days recording parameters for safety and function.

An inquiry was set up later to know the reasons for the accident, final report only pointed out accidental tempering. And as the INS Godavari sailed on into the new day, the crew knew that they could face whatever challenges lay ahead, knowing that they had each other's backs and that together, they were an unstoppable force to be reckoned with.

Seafarer's Symphony: Tale of Repair and Resilience

Vishal was by now a seasoned shipwright artificer engineer on the INS Godavari, a formidable frigate that cut through the waves with precision. His journey from a wide-eyed trainee to a hands-on expert had brought him face to face with the intricate dance of repair and maintenance tasks that defined his life aboard a naval vessel.

One of the most challenging assignments Vishal encountered was during a dry-docking operation. The ship's hull loomed above the waterline as it awaited maintenance in the dry dock facility. Vishal, equipped with his gears and a team of skilled technicians, descended into the cavernous space below the waterline to inspect the ship's hull. The underwater world was a realm of shadows and echoes, illuminated only by the glow of welding torches and the occasional beam of a flashlight. Vishal's expertise in hull repair and structural integrity came to the forefront as he meticulously oversees the ship's hull repair and maintenance by naval dockyard personals, ensuring it could withstand the harsh conditions of the open sea.

Godavari being a frontline ship, was equipped for creating citadel zones among compartments. It was designed to maintain gastight integrity within each zone to protect against air contamination when passing through a nuclear radiation affected area while at sea. Vishal, along with his team, ensured though periodic check and testing, that all components for ensuring it are in perfect condition. They ensured that gas tight doors, hatches and air intake and exhaust, mushroom heads seals were all intact, and the Air Filtration Unit was functioning flawlessly. Dockyard's Hull Inspection and Testing Unit carried out frequent checks and cleared it only if all found good. Responsibility weighed heavily on Vishal, knowing the role a perfect citadel played in the safety and security of the ship and its crew during crisis.

Hull damage control tasks became a routine part of Vishal's responsibilities. They would regularly conduct the mock exercises for ship side damages as a routine. Deck machinery and boat davits, essential for launching smaller boats for various operations, were under Vishal's vigilant care. Mechanical system checks, and structural integrity were his priorities. Each mechanism had to function seamlessly to guarantee the ship's readiness for any mission.

Vishal's journey aboard INS Godavari was a symphony of repair and resilience. The ship, a complex amalgamation of technology and strength, relied on the expertise of engineers like Vishal and many fellow artificers engineer be it electrical, marine or air to keep its heart beating. Vishal observed over a period his fellow artificers in the role of electrical & electronics engineer at work. Those who handle whether it was ships electrical power, radio & telecommunication, ships navigational equipment, air or underwater surveillance systems, weapon control system, Vishal observed all of them for their expertise with awe.

One day a news spread like a fire that Godavari will be sailing around the world for long six months across many nations. Every crew member was jubilant and looked forward to the mission. Vishal was apprehensive about the actual date as his marriage was planned in April 1986. Over few days it became clear that ship would most probably set sail in mid-May. He was relieved and started to prepare for the event.

An Artificer's Camaraderie

On INS Godavari, a formidable, guided missile frigate, a unique camaraderie flourished among five artificer engineers, each an expert in their distinct field. Rajiv Nair, the Radio and Communication expert, Iqbal Sharif specializing in underwater sonar technology, Krishnan, a marine engineer and engine room artificer, Kadir Ali an Electrical Power expert, and Vishal; ship's hull expert and shipwright artificer, formed an inseparable bond amidst the controlled chaos of their daily duties. At the end of each day, as the sun dipped below the horizon, casting a warm glow over the vast expanse of the sea, the five engineers would gather in a quiet cabin of the ship during free time to play games or share their stories. It became a ritual, a sanctuary where they could unwind, reflect, and bond over the laurels and ordeals of their respective departments.

Rajiv Nair, with his fingers dancing over the radio console, recounted the challenges of maintaining seamless communication in the ever-evolving landscape of naval technology. He spoke of the moments when swift and efficient communication had played a pivotal role in the success of the ship's operations. But he also shared the headaches of dealing with intricate systems, ensuring that every radio equipment was flawless. He was a constant member of wheelhouse operation team whenever the ship sailed.

Iqbal Sharif, a master of underwater acoustics and decoys, spoke passionately about the complexities of sonar technology. He detailed the triumphs of successfully detecting submarines during training exercises, the elation of outsmarting potential threats. Yet, he also spoke of the delicate balance required to differentiate between the cacophony of underwater sounds, avoiding false alarms that could lead to unnecessary tension.

Krishnan, a marine engineer and engine room artificer, delved into the intricacies of keeping the ship's heart—its engines—beating steadily. He talked of the countless hours spent in the belly of the ship, ensuring that ships propulsions and varied machineries operated with precision, see if shaft seals or bearings are not flooding the bilges. His stories oscillated between the satisfaction of a well-maintained engine room and the frustration of dealing with unexpected breakdowns.

Kadir Ali, an electrical artificer, with expertise in electrical power system, always shared his engineering stories in crisis, whether it was sudden blackouts or other malfunctioning in the power system, his expertise was highly valued and relied upon.

Finally, Vishal, the ship's Shipwright Artificer, shared tales of overseeing the construction and maintenance of the ship's structure and deck machineries. From repairing minor damages to orchestrating major overhauls during dry dockings, to monitoring ship's hull potential and cathodic protection, maintenance of ships piping systems and valves or the subject of ship's stability, his job was to ensure ship's seaworthiness. Vishal spoke of the satisfaction derived from the challenges of managing a team responsible for the ship's structural integrity.

They were all separated by two to three years in training batches and respected each other for their seniority. As they shared their stories, the five engineers found solace in the understanding glances of their comrades. The weight of their responsibilities, the challenges they faced daily, and the victories they celebrated became the ties that bound them. In those quiet moments, amidst the hum of the ship's engines and the distant sound of waves, they found not just colleagues but friends who shared a unique partnership forged through the demanding crucible of naval engineering.

INS Godavari sailed through the open sea, a floating testament to the collective expertise of Rajiv, Iqbal, Krishnan, Kadir and Vishal and other crew members. And as they faced the unknown challenges that lay ahead, they knew they could count on the strength of their camaraderie to weather any storm, both literally and figuratively, that the vast ocean might throw their way.

They would venture out together when away from base port to explore the places, and drink and dine together thus forming an inseparable bond. Together, they were not just colleagues, but partners united by a shared passion for adventure and exploration on the high seas.

Just into the Marriage- A Sad Parting

Vishal's heart was torn between duty and love as he stood in the doorway of his home, looking at Payal, the beautiful woman he had married just two weeks ago. Their long-distance love story of one years had been a whirlwind of romance and joy, but now a once-in-a-lifetime opportunity awaited Vishal, a journey that would take him away from his new bride for six long months. Vishal posted on a new frigate ship, was embarking on a diplomatic mission to showcase India's prowess in building large naval vessels. The voyage would span 22 ports in 18 countries across the globe, and Vishal felt a mix of pride and sadness as he prepared to leave his young wife behind.

Payal, understanding the significance of Vishal's mission, smiled through her tears. She was proud of her husband's service, its white uniform and the honour bestowed upon him. Vishal promised to stay connected through letters, and he reassured Payal that this journey was an opportunity that could not be missed. As Vishal boarded the train at New Delhi for rejoining the ship after his leave, he couldn't help but glance back at Payal, who stood there with a brave smile and tears in her eyes, waving him off. Within few days, the ship set on sail, and Vishal immersed himself in the responsibilities of his role as chief shipwright artificer. The days turned into weeks, and the frigate sailed through vast oceans, representing the strength and technological advancements of the Indian Navy.

Meanwhile, back home, Payal navigated the challenges of being a newlywed without her husband by her side. She missed Vishal deeply but found solace in their letter communication. As she managed the household and built connections with her new family, Payal patiently awaited Vishal's return.

Vishal, amidst his professional duties, often found himself reminiscing about the special moments he had shared with Payal. The camaraderie among the ship's crew helped ease the longing for home, and they forged bonds that transcended the seas they sailed. Throughout the diplomatic tour, the frigate made stops in diverse countries, showcasing the capabilities of Indian naval engineering. Vishal, proud to represent his country, worked tirelessly to ensure the ship's systems operated at peak performance. He shared stories of India's maritime achievements, fostering international cooperation and admiration for the country's naval prowess.

EXPLORING THE WORLD: A DIPLOMATIC MISSION

On International Voyage: A Dream Odyssey

The crisp sea air filled the deck of the Godavari as Vishal stood among the labyrinth of machinery, his eyes scanning the vast expanse of the frigate. A seasoned naval artificer engineer, Vishal and other fellow artificers took pride in the meticulous care of the ship's hull and machinery, ensuring it stood ready for any mission the navy entrusted it with. As the ship prepared for a six-month sea mission, Vishal knew the challenges ahead were as vast as the waters they would traverse.

The ship had a new commanding Officer Captain Pramanik, who had replaced Captain Rustomji few months ago. Dedicated team of ships engineers worked tirelessly to ensure every machinery was in perfect condition. The logistics for the ships long voyage were undertaken and completed by each department. From arranging spares of machineries to ration, ammunition, oils, and other essentials.

Beginning of an Unforgettable Voyage-Djibouti

In the spring of 1986, the naval ship INS Godavari departed, carrying a crew of above three hundreds with it on a memorable mission marked with diplomacy. Ships world voyage began from Bombay, as the Godavari set sail into the Arabian Sea. The ship cut through the Arabian Sea, setting sail on a mission that promised adventure and discovery. Their first destination was Djibouti, a small but picturesque nation nestled on the horn at northeastern coast of Africa.

The crew members were issued US dollars as foreign port allowance upon arrival at each port. This was to enable the crew to meet local expenses in the country of visit for shopping and dining. As Godavari approached the port of Djibouti, in Gulf of Aden, the crew admired the unique landscape that unfolded before them. The arid beauty of the region, with its vast deserts and rugged mountains, hinted at the rich tapestry of experiences that awaited them.

Their first day in Djibouti was dedicated to exploring the city itself. Vishal and his friends wandered through the lively markets, where the air was filled with the aromas of exotic spices, local delicacies, and the vibrant colours of fabrics. They engaged with the friendly Djiboutian locals, learning about the nation's history and traditions.

The following day, the crew set out to discover the natural wonders of Djibouti. They visited the breathtaking Lake Assal, one of the lowest points on earth and renowned for its high salt concentration. The stark beauty of the lake, surrounded by volcanic landscapes, left Vishal and his friends in awe. In the afternoon, they made their way to the Gulf of Tadjoura, where pristine beaches awaited. The soft sand and clear waters were an invitation to relax and unwind. Vishal and his friends revelled in the warmth of the sun, taking in the stunning views of the Red Sea on one side and the Gulf of Aden on the other.

On their final day in Djibouti, the crew explored the historic district of the capital, Djibouti City. They visited the charming European Quarter, a testament to the nation's colonial past, and the lively Afar market, where traders offered a variety of goods, from traditional crafts to spices. As the sun began to set on the third day, painting the Djiboutian sky with hues of orange and pink, Vishal and his friends' exchanged stories and laughter, relishing the memories they had made in this small but enchanting corner of the world.

The naval ship set sail once again, leaving Djibouti's shores behind. Vishal and friends, enriched by their three-day journey, carried the spirit of Djibouti with them. The diplomatic mission had not only strengthened ties between nations but had also allowed the crew to appreciate the beauty and warmth of a place.

Arrival at Port Suez

In the scorching summer of 1986, the naval ship INS Godavari, led by Captain Pramanik, embarked on voyage from Djibouti that would take them through the strategic Suez Canal. Their journey carried them, from Gulf of Aden to Red Sea to Gulf of Suez leading to the gateway between the continents at Port Suez.

As the INS Godavari approached Port Suez, the crew could see the bustling activity around the canal. The city, a vital hub for international maritime trade, hummed with energy and the promise of new adventures. Their stay at Port Suez was brief but filled with memorable experiences. After the ship docked, Captain Pramanik allowed his crew some well-deserved rest and relaxation. The sailors, who had been at sea, eagerly disembarked, ready to explore the surroundings.

The crew roamed through the lively streets of Port Suez, immersing themselves in the local culture. The air was filled with the enticing aroma of street food, and vendors offered colourful wares at every corner. Vishal and his comrades engaged with the locals, exchanging stories and laughter, bridging cultural gaps with a shared spirit of camaraderie. In the evening, the crew gathered at a local café to enjoy traditional Egyptian cuisine. The aromatic spices and exotic flavours were a delight to their senses. Over plates of koshari and falafel, they shared tales of their naval adventures and learned more about the vibrant life along the Suez Canal.

The following day, the crew had the opportunity to visit some historical landmarks, including the Suez Canal Authority building and the iconic lighthouse that guided ships through the canal. Vishal learnt the importance of the Suez Canal to global trade, and marvelled at the engineering that facilitated the passage of ships between the Mediterranean and the Red Sea.

As the INS Godavari prepared to navigate the Suez Canal, the crew bid farewell to the warm hospitality of Port Suez. The short stay had left an indelible mark on their journey, providing a glimpse into the rich history and culture of the region. The ship sailed through the Suez Canal, led in a flotilla of many ships piloted by a trained Master on a lead ship. The crew, now well-rested and invigorated by their time in Port Suez, cross through Great Bitter Lake in between, before entering the Mediterranean Sea to approach their next set of diplomatic missions at Sevastopol. The memories of their short stay in Egypt lingered, reminding them of the interconnectedness of the global maritime community and the shared bonds that transcend borders. The crew marvelled at the historic wonders of Egypt and the cultural richness of the African nations along the coast. Vishal witnessed the seamless transition as the ship navigated the narrow waterway, his team ready to face the challenges of the open sea.

As Godavari sailed Mediterranean Sea towards Black Sea, crossing through Bosporus Bay, the Turkish coast guard vessel was constant escort throughout via passing through Istanbul city and under the famous bridge connecting Asia and Europe. As ship crossed the bridge, the sight of iconic Blue Mosque on one side, a UNESCO world heritage site declared just a year back, could not be missed. A little later ship entered the black sea for Sevastopol.

Bridging Histories: INS Godavari in Sevastopol

In the spring of 1986, the INS Godavari, a proud frigate of the Indian Navy, sailed into the historic naval port of Sevastopol, then part of Crimea in Ukraine in the Black Sea, marking the beginning of a historic journey into the heart of the undivided USSR. The crew, adorned in their ceremonial uniforms, stood with a mix of curiosity and reverence as the ship approached the port that had witnessed centuries of maritime history.

Sevastopol, a city now held by Russia, with a rich tapestry of stories etched into its shores, welcomed the Godavari with open arms. The port was home to many advance front-line ships and submarines of the Soviet navy. As the ship docked, the crew exclaimed at the grandeur of the city, its architectural marvels and naval infrastructure steeped in a legacy that dated back to the Crimean War. The significance of Sevastopol was not lost on the Indian crew. The city had withstood the ravages of war, including the infamous Siege of Sevastopol during World War II, where the Soviet Union defended the port against the German and Romanian forces for a staggering 250 days. The scars of that conflict still lingered in the city's landscape, a testament to the resilience of its people.

As the Indian crew disembarked, they were greeted by their Soviet counterparts, creating an atmosphere of camaraderie that transcended the political tensions of the time. The exchange of naval expertise and cultural insights fostered a sense of unity among the sailors, bridging the gap between two distant nations. Sevastopol's historic significance extended beyond military exploits. The city was home to the ruins of Chersonesus, an ancient Greek colony dating back to the 5th century BC. The crew of the Godavari explored these archaeological wonders, standing amidst the remnants of an ancient civilization that had once thrived on the shores of the Black Sea.

School children's group adoring uniform came in hordes to visit the Indian ship. The visit culminated in a grand reception, where Indian and Soviet officers exchanged toasts, celebrating the bonds of friendship and maritime heritage that connected their nations. The crews shared stories of their naval traditions, highlighting the similarities that bound them despite their geographical and political differences.

As the INS Godavari set sail from Sevastopol, the ship's crew carried with them not only the memories of a historic visit but also a deep appreciation for the resilience and shared history that united nations across the seas. Godavari sailed back into Bay of Bosphorus through Istanbul once again on its return trip and through the Mediterranean towards Algiers port in Algeria.

Arrival at Port City Algiers, Algeria

In the summer of 1986, the naval ship Godavari, docked at the historic port city of Algiers in Algeria. The crew, eager to explore the cultural riches of North Africa, looked forward to a two-day visit filled with adventure and discovery. As the ship's gangway lowered onto the pier, Vishal and his fellow crewmates disembarked onto the bustling streets of Algiers. The city, with its blend of French and Arabic influences, beckoned them to uncover its hidden gems.

Their first stop was the iconic Kasbah of Algiers, a UNESCO World Heritage site. Narrow alleyways wound through this ancient citadel, leading the crew past whitewashed buildings adorned with vibrant blue doors and wrought-iron balconies. They explored the intricate mosaics of the Great Mosque, marvelling at the architectural splendour that spoke of centuries of history.

Next on their itinerary was a visit to the Notre-Dame, a majestic basilica perched on a hill overlooking the Mediterranean. The crew ascended the steps, taking in panoramic views of Algiers and the sparkling sea below. Inside the basilica, they admired the stunning stained-glass windows and intricate artwork, a testament to the city's diverse cultural heritage. For a taste of local life, Vishal and his friends ventured into the heart of Algiers' markets. The crew engaged with locals, practicing a few phrases in Arabic and exchanging smiles that bridged language barriers. In the evening, the crew dined at a traditional Algerian restaurant, savouring couscous, tagines, and flavourful grilled meats. The rhythmic sounds of live music filled the air, creating an ambiance of celebration that resonated with the warmth of Algerian hospitality.

The crew set out to explore the modern side of Algiers on following day. They strolled along the wide boulevards of the city centre, lined with French colonial architecture and bustling with urban life. The Jardin, a botanical garden established during the French colonial era, offered a tranquil escape with its lush greenery and exotic plant species.

On third day as INS Godavari prepared to depart from Algiers, Vishal and his crewmates gathered on the ship's deck, their hearts filled with gratitude for the memorable two days they had spent in this captivating city. The diplomatic mission had allowed the crew to appreciate the beauty and warmth of Algiers, a place that had left an indelible mark on their journey across the seas.

Ponta Del Gada, Azores, Portugal

In the mid-Atlantic, amidst the vastness of the ocean, Godavari charted a course towards Ponta Delgada, a picturesque Portuguese territory nestled on the island of São Miguel in the Azores. It is an archipelago composed of nine volcanic islands in the Macaronesia region of the North Atlantic Ocean, about 800 nautical miles west of Lisbon.

Vishal, along with his fellow engineers, eagerly anticipated the stopover, a respite from the routine of naval duties. As the ship glided into the calm waters of Ponta Delgada, the crew admired the lush green landscapes and the charming architecture that adorned the island. The air was crisp and invigorating, a stark contrast to the open sea that surrounded them for days. Vishal and his fellow engineers, clad in their navy whites and black blazers, disembarked onto the welcoming shores, ready to explore.

The excursion began with a visit to the historic town centre, where cobbled streets led to quaint squares surrounded by pastel-coloured buildings. Vishal and his companions admired the intricate Portuguese tilework that adorned many facades, a testament to the island's rich cultural heritage. The aroma of local delicacies wafted through the air, enticing the crew to indulge in traditional Azorean cuisine. The island's natural wonders beckoned next, and the crew embarked on a journey to the Sete Cidades, a stunning twin-lake crater surrounded by rolling hills. As they stood on the lookout point, Vishal and his fellow friends were captivated by the breathtaking views of the azure and emerald lakes, framed by the lush landscape.

Furnas volcano a volcanic site lies at the eastern end of Sao Miguel Island, immediately west of the older Nordeste shield volcano and its Povoaçao caldera. There are at least two calderas, a large cauldron, a hollow like depression formed by emptying of magma chamber, a younger one that is 6-km wide and a larger older one that is less topographically distinct. Its volcanic activity dates back about 100,000 years. Two historical eruptions have occurred, one sometime between 1439 and 1443 and the other in 1630. The latter was one of the largest Holocene explosive eruptions in the Azores and caused significant damage and fatalities. Volcanic complex of Furnas is known for its thermal waters that form pools of medicinal and natural water pools. The hot steam from ground at many places are seen all around that creates a scenic ambience amid hill terrain. This volcano is located within the Azores, a UNESCO Global Geopark property.

In the evening, the crew gathered at a local eatery, where traditional folk music filled the air, and the aroma of freshly caught seafood teased their senses. Vishal and his fellow engineers savoured the unique blend of Portuguese and Azorean flavours, forging memories over shared drinks and meals.

The visit to Ponta Delgada became a cherished interlude for the crew of the Godavari. As they bid farewell to the island and set sail once again, the friendship forged on the shores of São Miguel lingered among the crew. The mid-Atlantic oasis had not only provided a scenic respite but had also become a chapter in the seafaring tales of Vishal and his fellow engineers, etched in the logbook of their maritime adventures.

Sailing the Liberty Seas: Historic US Voyage

As ship departed port of Ponta Del Gada, and the Indian frigate Godavari re commenced on a historic journey across the Atlantic, bound for the United States. Under the command of Captain Pramanik, the ship's crew was eager for the unique opportunity to visit the shores of the USA, a nation with which India shared both diplomatic ties and a rich maritime history.

Their first port of call was Norfolk, a bustling naval port in Virginia. As the Godavari docked, the American and Indian flags fluttered side by side, symbolizing the friendship between the two nations. The mighty nuclear powered Aircraft Carriers USS Enterprise and USS Nimitz of US Navy and other frontline warships berthed nearby was a sight far too impressive. The crew of the Godavari was welcomed with open arms, fostering a cultural exchange that bridged the gap between the two naval forces.

From Norfolk, the Godavari set sail to Alexandria in Washington, where they were greeted by picturesque views of the Potomac River. The crew took in the historic landmarks of the nation's capital, fostering friendships that transcended borders. The Indian sailors marvelled at the sights, appreciating the rich history and cultural diversity of the United States. The visit to White House, Capitol Hill, Central Park, Washington Memorial, Aerospace Museum, and market visit by metro trains were some of the highlights of visit.

The pinnacle of their journey awaited them in New York City, where INS Godavari would participate in an International Naval Review on July 4th, the United States' Independence Day. President Ronald Reagan was scheduled to preside over the event with participation of close to sixty countries representing their flag, marking it as a momentous occasion for all participating countries.

As the Godavari sailed into New York Harbor, the iconic skyline of Manhattan came into view. The view of twin towers was most prominent in the horizon from jetty where Godavari was berthed. The sailors were in awe of the Statue of Liberty, standing tall and proud after undergoing a significant renovation. The harbour sparkled with anticipation as ships from various nations assembled for the International Naval Review.

On the morning of July 4th, 1986, the sun rose over New York Harbor, casting a golden glow on the waters. The INS Godavari, resplendent and dressed in its naval regalia, joined the international fleet. President Ronald Reagan, aboard a small naval vessel sailed past, took the salute and reviewed while saluting back to the participating navies, all anchored and lined up at designated position. The event was preceded by large flotilla of sail ships of all sizes, sailed and crossed channel toward sea through the New York harbour. It was a spectacular sight to watch with pomp and show associated with the Independence Day function. Once the Presidential review was concluded, harbour was filled with boat of all sizes with citizens cheering, singing and dancing amid music.

After the Naval Review, ship's Captain, and a select group of crews from the Godavari proceeded on a visit to the newly renovated Statue of Liberty. Against the backdrop of Lady Liberty, a symbol of freedom and friendship, an officer from US Navy spoke of the shared values that bound the two nations.

During four days of stay, ship's crew went around the bustling city exploring famous areas of New York city. As the sun set over the New York skyline, casting a glow over the harbour, the crew of the Godavari reflected on their journey with a sense of awe and gratitude. They had travelled thousands of miles, forging bonds of friendship and camaraderie with their American allies and leaving behind memories that would last a lifetime. Their visit of two weeks to USA was full of cherished memories.

And as they sailed into the sunset, bound for new horizons and new adventures, they carried with them the spirit of liberty and the hope for a brighter future for all mankind. For in the end, it was not just a journey across the sea, but a journey of the heart, one that would be remembered for generations to come. The journey had left an indelible mark on the sailors who had the privilege of participating in this remarkable chapter of Indian naval history. As they sailed toward next port of call, the glimpses of Miami shore and skyline on the way from sea filled up excitement in the journey ahead.

Country of Great Revolution- Havana, Cuba

The Indian sailor's heart swelled with a mix of astonishment and gratitude as Indian Naval Ship slowly approached the port of Havana, Cuba after leaving New York. The sight of the vibrant city, with its colourful buildings and lively atmosphere, added an extra layer of excitement to the anticipation building within him.

As the ship docked, the crew members donned their uniforms with a sense of pride, eager to represent their country on foreign soil. Ship was opened for the public to visit and see. An impressive crowd including school Childrens had come to the jetty to board the Indian naval ship and go around accompanied by crew. The language was a barrier but nevertheless, message was friendship was conveyed and reciprocated.

Next day, the air buzzed with a palpable sense of curiosity as they awaited the special guest rumoured to be arriving. Whispers among the crew hinted at the possibility of an esteemed visitor, but none could have anticipated the grandeur of the welcome that awaited them. Suddenly, the news spread like wildfire throughout the ship – President Fidel Castro himself was on his way to visit the ship and meet the Indian crew. The embassy staff and ship's crew made all efforts to welcome their distinguished guest. The sailor's heart raced with a mix of honour and disbelief. It was a rare and unforgettable moment for the crew of the Indian ship, a gesture of friendship that transcended borders.

As the President's motorcade approached the dock, the ship's crew led by commanding officer stood at attention on the deck, with a mix of nerves and pride surging through. The arrival of President Fidel Castro was not just an event; it was a historic meeting that would be etched in their memories forever. The moment President Castro stepped onto the ship; the atmosphere shifted. The sailor admired at the charismatic leader in his iconic olive-green uniform, his beard a symbol of revolutionary ideals. A warm breeze carried the scent of the sea, blending with the rich aroma of Cuban soil. The sailor couldn't help but feel a connection between the two nations, oceans apart yet united in that singular moment.

President Castro, with a twinkle in his eye, greeted the crew members with a firm handshake and a smile. The sailors, standing tall and proud, exchanged pleasantries with the esteemed leader, feeling a sense of camaraderie that transcended language barriers. The President's genuine warmth created an atmosphere of goodwill, and the sailor couldn't help but be overwhelmed by the hospitality extended to them. Commanding officer led the President inside to VIP room and exchanged pleasantries over session of tea and coffee. As a token of friendship, President Castro presented the crew with a truckload of fresh, tropical fruits – a gesture that spoke volumes. The sailor, eyes wide with gratitude, marvelled at the colourful array of pineapples, mangoes, bananas, and many tinned fruits. It was a symbolic offering that bridged the gap between cultures, a gesture that transcended diplomatic formalities.

In that moment, as the sailor savoured the taste of Cuban fruits and exchanged laughs with his fellow crew members, they realized the profound impact of this unexpected encounter. The meeting with President Fidel Castro wasn't just a diplomatic formality; it was a shared celebration of the sea's unifying spirit, connecting sailors from distant lands in a moment of genuine friendship and goodwill. A gala dinner was also organised by the Cuban community next day, in coordination with embassy, to honour and treat their guests. Around Seventy Indian crew members attended the function and were humbled by the gesture and took back fond memories.

Caribbean Call - Sound of Reggae at Kingston, Jamaica

From Cuba, Indian naval ship Godavari arrived at the vibrant port of Kingston in Jamaica. Vishal and other crew, eagerly disembarked, ready to immerse themselves in the rich culture and warm hospitality of this Caribbean Island nation. On duty crew, other than routine responsibility, were engaged in showcasing the ship to visiting local citizens. Jamaica had considerable Indian population and they were over excited to meet and mingle with Indian crew of the ship.

As they stepped onto Jamaican soil, the crew was greeted by the rhythmic beats of reggae music drifting through the air. The colourful streets of Kingston beckoned, lined with bustling markets and vibrant murals depicting the island's history and heritage. Their first stop was the iconic Bob Marley Museum, a tribute to Jamaica's most famous musician and reggae legend. Vishal and his friends explored the museum's exhibits, learning about Marley's life and legacy, and feeling the spirit of reggae music pulsating through their veins. They ventured into the heart of Kingston's markets, where vendors sold everything from fresh fruits and spices to handmade crafts and souvenirs. The crew haggled with the locals, practicing their Jamaican patois, and revelling in the lively atmosphere of the market.

Next day, Vishal and his friends sought refuge from the heat in the cool waters of Kingston's beaches. They spent hours lounging on the sandy shores, soaking up the Caribbean sun and taking in the breathtaking views of the turquoise sea. In the evening, they dined at a local restaurant, indulging in Jamaican specialties such as jerk chicken and saltfish, and fried plantains. They washed down their meal with glasses of refreshing coconut water, beer and sampled the island's famous Jamaican rum cocktails, feeling the cares of the world melt away in the warmth of Jamaican hospitality.

Their time in Kingston was a whirlwind of adventure and discovery, filled with laughter, music, and unforgettable experiences. As the INS Godavari prepared to depart from Jamaica, Indian crew, their hearts full of gratitude for the memories they had made on this tropical paradise. The diplomatic mission had brought them to Kingston, but it was the spirit of Jamaica and its people that had truly captured their hearts. Next port of call was Port of Spain in Trinidad.

Steel Drum Rhythm - Port of Spain, Trinidad & Tobago

In the August of 1986, the naval ship INS Godavari, docked at the bustling Port of Spain in Trinidad and Tobago. Vishal, his friends, and other fellow crew were eager to explore the vibrant culture and warm hospitality of this Caribbean gem. As they stepped off the ship and onto Trinidadian soil, they were greeted by the sounds of steel drums and the sweet scent of tropical flowers. The colourful streets of Port of

Spain beckoned, inviting the crew to immerse themselves in the lively atmosphere of the city.

They explored the historic sites of Port of Spain, including the majestic Red House and the iconic Queen's Park Savannah. They appreciated its architecture and learned about the rich history of Trinidad and Tobago. But perhaps the highlight of their visit came when INS Godavari's team was invited to play a friendly cricket match against the West Indies Navy cricket team at the famous Queen's Park Oval. Cricket, the most liked sport, both in India and the West Indies, brought the two naval teams together in a spirit of friendly competition. Vishal, an avid cricketer was integral part of the Godavari's team which played with determination and skill. The match was played under the warm Caribbean sun, with spectators cheering from the stands and the sounds of laughter filling the air. In the end, it was not the outcome of the match that mattered, but the bonds of friendship forged between the two teams. After the game, both teams celebrated the event over meal, swapping stories and jokes.

Later, Vishal and his group of friends were privately hosted by Indian community. Mrs Ramola and family who owned Bata's franchise there, invited group at their home over dinner. There was natural bonding at display from both sides as they shared interesting news and stories from their respective nation. But the common thread was cricket, but they would not tolerate any criticism of west indies team particularly the younger lot.

As the INS Godavari prepared to depart from Port of Spain, Vishal and his friends looked back on their time in Trinidad with fondness and gratitude. The Caribbean hospitality and warmth they had experienced had left an indelible mark on their journey, reminding them of the power of friendship and camaraderie, both on and off the cricket field. They were now headed to Georgetown in Guyana,

Garden city of the Caribbean - Georgetown, Guyana

Next port of call for Godavari was the vibrant port of Georgetown in Guyana, city founded as a settlement by the British in 1781 and largely built by the French. As ship docked alongside jetty at port, crew members eagerly stepped ashore, ready to explore the rich culture and warm hospitality of this South American nation. This nation also had vast population of Indians whose forefathers were settled here by Britishers for farming.

Georgetown, with its colonial architecture and diverse population, unfolded before the crew like a canvas painted with colours of history and tradition. The lively streets beckoned, lined with markets, historic buildings, and the lively chatter of locals. Their first stop was the Stabroek Market, a bustling hub of activity where vendors sold fresh produce, handmade crafts, and an array of spices. Vishal and his friends mingled with the locals, exchanging smiles and stories, creating an instant connection that transcended cultural boundaries.

Next, they explored the iconic wooden St. George's Cathedral, a testament to Guyana's colonial past. The intricate architecture and serene atmosphere provided a moment of reflection amid the vibrant energy of the city. As the crew strolled through the historic districts of Georgetown, they encountered the vibrant blend of cultures that defined Guyana. The crew members engaged with locals, learning about the traditions and customs that made this nation unique. In the evening, Vishal and his friends ventured to the famous Seawall, a picturesque promenade along the Atlantic Ocean. They marvelled at the stunning sunset, its hues reflecting off the water, as they enjoyed the soothing sounds of the waves and the cool sea breeze.

During next day, as a gesture of cultural exchange, the Godavari hosted a dinner aboard for Guyanese naval officers and crew. The exchange of stories and the sharing of traditional dishes from both nations strengthened the ties of friendship between the two naval forces. Some of the Indian crew were privately hosted over dinner by Indian natives at their homes in groups. There was natural bonding at display and ship's crew loved all of it. As the ship prepared to depart from Georgetown, Vishal and his friends reflected on their time in Guyana with gratitude. The warmth of the people, the vibrant culture, and the shared moments of laughter and connection had left an indelible mark on their hearts.

The crew was all set for departure as Godavari prepared to cast off from the bustling port of Georgetown, Guyana, in afternoon but the gust of wind was particularly strong. The forceful winds tested the vessel's mooring lines, and amidst the sounds of creaking metal and the churning waters, disaster struck. The starboard capstan shaft sheared like a slice, rendering it totally dysfunctional. Vishal, along with his senior Pushkar, quickly assessed the situation and realized the severity of the damage. With one capstan disabled, the ship faced a critical challenge. Casting off from the port required the functionality of both capstans for handling of mooring and anchoring purpose. In the interim, the crew improvised to manage the departure from Georgetown. More tugboats were called in to assist, and the ship slowly maneuverer away from the dock with tug assistance. The temporary solution allowed INS Godavari to continue its journey, albeit with handicap of one anchor.

Time was of the essence as the ship's next destination of port Recife in Brazil awaited. Meanwhile, ship learnt about the decision of air freighting of new capstan shaft from Bombay to the next port of call. The time was constraint, and it was only possible to receive new shaft by the time ship arrives at Accra in Ghana, West Africa.

A 16th Century City - Recife, Brazil

The INS Godavari, a majestic frigate of the Indian Navy, sailed into the vibrant port of Recife in Brazil, greeted by the warm embrace of the tropical sun and the rhythmic beats of Brazilian music. As the ship docked, the crew eagerly anticipated their time ashore, eager to explore the rich culture and vibrant atmosphere of this exotic destination. No sooner had the gangway been lowered that beautiful Brazilian girl in groups appeared around the dock, their smiles as radiant as the sun itself. Drawn by the allure of the Indian crew, they eagerly approached the ship, their laughter and playful banter filling the air. On the jetty, large crowd showed up to welcome and later boarded the ship to visit. Crowd showed no signs of slowing down as guests visited, the warm sea breeze carrying the scent of adventure and friendship.

The sailors, delighted by the unexpected attention, welcomed guest aboard with open arms, eager to share their adventure with newfound friends. Together, they set off to explore the bustling markets and lively streets of Recife in evening, the girls leading the way with their infectious energy and zest for life. Amidst the colourful stalls and vibrant ambiance of the market, the group indulged in local delicacies and exotic drinks, savouring the flavours of Brazil, and sharing laughs. The language barrier proved to be no obstacle as gestures and smiles easily bridged the gap between cultures.

As the day turned into night, the festivities continued as the crew and their Brazilian companions danced under the stars, their laughter echoing through the streets of Recife. With each step and twirl, bonds were forged, transcending language and nationality. The night was alive with music and laughter as the sailors and their newfound friends revelled in the magic of the moment.

Next day, Vishal and friends decided to explore the long pristine beaches of Brazil. Boa Viagem Beach is the most famous in Recife and has a great structure for tourists. The place was quite busy; the weather was favourable; beach was crowded with beachgoers, people either swimming or relaxing. This beach had warm, greenish waters, providing not only a good dip in the sea but also an excellent background for the eyes. The strip of sand was seven kilometres lined with coconut trees. On the sidewalk there are kiosks that sell drinks & snacks and, on the sands, street vendors. Boa Viagem beach is lined with tall apartments, modern hotels, and restaurants, had relatively weak waves because the shore is sheltered by a large coral reef.

In the morning next day, as the sun began to rise over the horizon, casting its golden glow upon the tranquil waters of the port, the crew of the INS Godavari bid farewell to their Brazilian companions, their hearts filled with memories of a day filled with laughter, friendship, and adventure. As the ship set sail once more, leaving the port of Recife behind, the sailors knew that they would carry the spirit of Brazil with them wherever their journey took them. And as they sailed into the endless expanse of the ocean, they knew that the bonds of friendship forged on that fateful day would endure.

A Picturesque Coastal City- Accra, Ghana

Ship sailed from Recife in Brazil for the next part of the voyage and entered first African nation. The INS Godavari was docked in the bustling port of Accra, Ghana. The Indian Navy had sent the ship on a diplomatic and friendly mission to strengthen diplomatic ties, and Vishal was excited to be a part of this historic voyage.

Vishal's fellow shipmate joined him in this adventure. Together, they were tasked with engaging with local populations, visiting important places, and fostering goodwill during their three-day stay in each city.

Upon reaching the port of Accra port in Ghana, the new capstan shaft awaited installation. However, unforeseen delays in customs clearance and logistical challenges prolonged the wait. Frustration mounted as precious days slipped away, impacting the ship's schedule. Ships commanding officer, determined to overcome the setbacks, reached out to the Indian mission in Ghana, seeking assistance in expediting the customs process. Their diplomatic intervention proved crucial, and the new capstan shaft was cleared and received on ship.

With the replacement shaft in hand, Vishal and his team worked tirelessly to get the capstan operational. The repairs were meticulous, requiring precision and expertise. The crew laboured around the clock, driven by a sense of duty and commitment to getting INS Godavari back to full operational capacity. However, a new challenge emerged – A metal sleeve was required to be hot pushed on to the shaft and needed specialized tools. The hydraulic pressing machine were not readily available in the port. Ship's Commanding officer decided to sail ahead nevertheless as planned and decided to complete the task at their next port of call Lagos in Nigeria.

Accra welcomed them with warm smiles and vibrant colours. The city's markets were alive with the sounds of haggling and the aromas of local spices. Vishal and friends spent their first day exploring the historic Jamestown district, where they admired the colonial architecture and interacted with the friendly locals.

The following day, they visited the Kwame Nkrumah Mausoleum, paying homage to Ghana's first President. The visit turned into a cultural exchange, as Vishal and other shared stories about Indian history and traditions, and the Ghanaians reciprocated with tales of their struggle for independence. As the sun set over Accra, the naval crew joined the locals in a traditional dance at the Arts Centre, forging bonds that transcended borders.

The INS Godavari set sail for Lagos, Nigeria, next morning where a new chapter awaited them.

Across Gulf of Guinea - Lagos, Nigeria

As the sprawling city greeted them with its energy and diversity on arrival, ship's crew immersed themselves in Nigeria's rich cultural heritage at the National Museum. The museum's artifacts and exhibitions provided insights into the nation's history and art. The largest city of Nigeria, sprawls inland from Gulf of Guinea across Lagos lagoon. Crew immersed themselves at Freedom Park, once a colonial era prison.

However, Vishal had his priority clearly set to get the capstan operational by any means. He resourceful and adaptable, reached out to the Nigerian Navy, where he had few Nigerian friends from training days in India. They generously offered to support. The Nigerian Naval dockyard in Lagos provided the necessary machine, tools, expertise, and a conducive environment for the final stages of the repair. Collaborating with their Nigerian counterparts, Vishal and team successfully installed the new capstan shaft. The repaired capstan underwent testing to ensure its resilience under heavy forces. As the machinery roared back to life, a collective sigh of relief resonated among the crew.

The INS Godavari, once again fully operational, set sail from Lagos with a profound sense of accomplishment. The challenges faced in Georgetown and the subsequent repairs in Ghana and Nigeria had tested the crew's mettle. Yet, through determination, collaboration, and unwavering dedication, technical team had overcome adversity, ensuring the ship's continued mission, and showcasing the resilience and strength of naval cooperation across borders.

While Vishal and team were occupied with technical issue, others went around the city and places of interest to see around. The final day in Lagos was dedicated to a diplomatic luncheon, attended by officials from both countries.

As the INS Godavari sailed away from the Lagos, Vishal and others reflected on their memorable journey. The friendships formed, the cultural exchanges, and the diplomatic ties strengthened during those six days in Accra and Lagos that transcended naval missions, leaving behind a legacy of unity and cooperation between India and the vibrant nations of West Africa.

A Port City with Seafront Promenade - Luanda, Angola

INS Godavari entered Angola next, crew found themselves in the vibrant city of Luanda. Their visit was part of a mission, aimed at fostering goodwill and strengthening ties between India and Angola. Excitement buzzed through the air as they prepared to explore the sights and sounds of this bustling African city.

Their first stop was the historic Fortaleza Miguel, a formidable fortress that stood as a testament to Angola's colonial past. Vishal and his friends went around to see the sturdy walls and imposing cannons, imagining the battles that had once been fought within its confines. From the ramparts, they gazed out over the sparkling waters of the Atlantic Ocean, taking in the breathtaking views of Luanda's coastline.

Next, they ventured into the heart of the city, where the colourful markets of Roque Santeria awaited them. The narrow alleyways were lined with stalls overflowing with fresh produce, vibrant fabrics, and handcrafted souvenirs. Vishal found himself drawn to the lively atmosphere, as vendors called out to passersby and bargaining ensued over the price of goods. As they wandered through the market, they sampled local delicacies such as grilled fish, fried plantains, and spicy piri piri sauce. They engaged in friendly banter with the Angolan vendors, exchanging stories and laughter as they explored the rich tapestry of culture and tradition that permeated every corner of the market.

Next day, their first stop was the Agostinho Neto Mausoleum, a solemn tribute to Angola's first President. Here, amidst the serene gardens and towering statues, Vishal and his friends paid their respects to a man who had played a pivotal role in shaping the nation's history. In the heart of Luanda, the sailors discovered the lively atmosphere of the Largo do Ambientes, a central square where locals gathered for socializing and entertainment. They joined in the festivities, absorbing the rhythms of traditional music and dance that echoed through the streets.

As the day ended, Vishal and his other friends returned to the ship, their hearts full of memories from their time in Luanda.

A Sea Voyage from Angola to Mozambique

In October 1986, INS Godavari was now on its sea voyage from Luanda in Angola to Maputo in Mozambique. The journey could have been relatively short, but diplomatic constraints imposed by the prevailing apartheid regime in South Africa meant that the ship had to steer clear of Namibia and the South African coast.

As the ship left the shores of Angola, Vishal couldn't help but feel a sense of anticipation for the upcoming visit to Mozambique. The crew aboard the INS Godavari, understanding the geopolitical complexities that dictated their course. Days turned into nights, and the open sea stretched endlessly before them. Vishal, usually immersed in the sound at sea and the routine of naval life, now found himself with more time on his hands. He took advantage of this unplanned respite to engage in conversations with fellow crew members, sharing stories and experiences. The ship became a floating community, with crew finding solace in camaraderie. Vishal, the naval engineer, spent his spare hours not only maintaining the ship's machinery but also participated in indoor games and impromptu gatherings where crew shared their tales.

As Godavari sailed through the vastness of Atlantic Ocean towards the Indian Ocean, around the Cape of Good Hope, the crew admired the beauty of the open sea, and watched coastal land around South Africa. They witnessed breathtaking sunsets and stared in awe at the star-studded night sky, far away from the city lights that usually obscured such celestial displays.

As Godavari reached the shores of Maputo, the crew having weathered the extended voyage with resilience and camaraderie, eagerly disembarked to explore Mozambique's capital. The challenges faced during the journey only strengthened the bonds among the naval personnel, turning what could have been a mundane voyage into an adventure of shared stories and newfound friendships.

Once arrived in Maputo, Vishal couldn't help but appreciate the resilience of the crew and the unique camaraderie that had developed during their unexpected voyage. The diplomatic constraints that altered their course had inadvertently created an indelible chapter in the journey of the INS Godavari and its crew.

Life at Maputo, Mozambique

Vishal, aboard the INS Godavari, found himself amidst the vibrant cityscape of Maputo, Mozambique. The ship's diplomatic visit aimed to strengthen friendly ties between two nations, and Vishal was eager to explore the cultural richness of this African nation.

As the ship docked in Maputo's harbour, Vishal and his fellow crew members disembarked, greeted by the warm breeze and the sounds of bustling activity. Their first stop was the iconic Maputo Railway Station, a stunning example of colonial-era architecture adorned with intricate wrought-iron decorations. Vishal marvelled at the grandeur of the building, a symbol of Mozambique's complex history.

Next, they ventured into the heart of the city, where they explored the vibrant markets and lively streets. Vishal was struck by the kaleidoscope of colours and the exotic aromas of street food that filled the air. The crew mingled with the locals, exchanging smiles and gestures of goodwill despite the language barrier. Their journey continued to the historic Fortaleza de Maputo, a 19th-century fortress overlooking the Indian Ocean. Vishal and his friends wandered through the stone walls, imagining the battles that had been fought there centuries ago. From the ramparts, they gazed out over the sparkling waters, feeling a sense of awe at the beauty of Mozambique's coastline.

In the afternoon, they visited the bustling FEIMA Arts and Crafts Market, where local artisans showcased their handcrafted goods. Vishal admired the intricate wood carvings, colourful textiles, and beaded jewellery on display, each item a testament to Mozambique's rich artistic heritage. As the day ended, Vishal and his fellow crew members were invited to a traditional Mozambican feast hosted by local dignitaries. They were treated to a sumptuous spread of grilled seafood, spicy peri-peri chicken, and flavourful rice dishes.

Throughout their visit to Maputo, Vishal and his friends were struck by the warmth and hospitality of the Mozambican people. Despite the challenges faced by the nation, their spirit remained resilient, and their generosity left a lasting impression on the crew of the INS Godavari. As the ship prepared to depart from Maputo, Vishal reflected on the day's experiences with gratitude. The diplomatic mission had not only strengthened ties between India and Mozambique but had also provided Vishal and his fellow crew members with a deeper appreciation for the beauty and diversity of the world beyond their own shores.

Seychelles, an Indian Ocean Archipelago

After an eventful sailing from Maputo, Mozambique, the crew of the Godavari found themselves sailing into the enchanting waters surrounding the picturesque islands of Seychelles. Vishal and his fellow crew members were eager as always to explore the natural beauty and vibrant culture of this tropical paradise. As the ship anchored in the harbour of Victoria, the capital city of Seychelles, Vishal and his comrades were greeted by the sight of swaying palm trees and pristine white beaches stretching out before them. The turquoise waters lapped gently against the shore, inviting them to immerse themselves in the island's tranquil ambiance.

With their duties temporarily put on hold, Vishal and friends wasted no time in venturing ashore to explore all that Seychelles had to offer. They began their adventure with a visit to the vibrant Selwyn-Clarke Market, where the air was filled with the fragrant aroma of exotic spices and tropical fruits. They mingled with the locals, sampling freshly caught seafood and bargaining for souvenirs to take home as mementos of their visit. Eager to discover the natural wonders of the island, Vishal and his companions embarked on a trek through the lush Seychellois National Park. They followed winding trails that led them through dense forests and past cascading waterfalls, marvelling at the diverse flora and fauna that surrounded them. From panoramic viewpoints, they gazed out over the emerald, green landscape, dotted with granite peaks and hidden coves. Their outing concluded with a visit to Beau Vallon, where the crew joined locals and fellow tourists in a lively beachside celebration. The rhythmic beats of traditional music filled the air as Seychellois and visitors alike danced under the starlit sky, creating memories that would last a lifetime.

Next day, Vishal and his companions set their sights on the pristine beaches that Seychelles is renowned for. They chose Anse Lazio, a breathtaking stretch of white sand framed by turquoise waters and granite boulders. The crew basked in the sun, swam in the crystal-clear sea, and revelled in the sheer beauty of their surroundings. That evening, Vishal and his fellow friends gathered on the deck of the Godavari; their hearts full of gratitude for the unforgettable day they had shared in Seychelles.

As the ship prepared to set sail once more, but this time back to home port Bombay, they knew that their memories of this tropical oasis would stay with them forever, a reminder of the beauty and wonder that awaited them on their maritime adventures.

Beginning of a Worldwide Trip of INS Godavari

Godavari Passing through the Suez Canal, Egypt

Godavari Crossing Bay of Bosphorus, Istanbul, Turkey towards Black Sea

Godavari's visit of Sevastopol, Russia (then USSR)

Visitors and School Childrens flocked the ship.

Godavari on arrival berthed at port Algiers, Algeria.

Alongside Sea King Helicopter on the deck of Godavari

at Ponta Del Gada, Purtgal

Furnaco at Ponta Del Gada

At Norfolk Waterfront, USA

Celebration at New York Harbour for US Independence Day- 04 July 1986

On arrival at New York Harbour

Godavari Ship on Anchorage at New York

(for International Fleet Review by US President Ronald Reagan)

At official Reception for Indian Crew in Havana, Cuba

Godavari Ship at Havana, Cuba   Local Caribbean Music, Havana

At Havana City tour

Childrens on board ship Godavari at Havana, Cuba

At Santa Maria Beach, Havana, Cuba

Local crowd on ships arrival at Caribbean Port of Kingston, Jamaica

An Indian Doctor's family on Visit to Godavari at Kingston

Free time at Ocho Rio Beach, Kingston

Ocho Rio Beach at Kingston, Jamaica Jamaica

Ocho Rio Waterfall, Kingston

City tour of Luanda, Angola

Journey Back Home, Bombay

As the Godavari sailed back into Bombay, Vishal couldn't help but feel a swell of pride. The frigate had successfully completed its mission, a testament to the dedication and skill of the operational and engineering crew on board commanded by an experienced captain. Vishal looked out at the city lights, knowing that the journey had not only strengthened the Godavari but also forged bonds of friendship and cooperation with nations across the globe.

The voyage of the Godavari was more than a sea mission; it was an odyssey that showcased the prowess of naval engineering, the resilience of an Indian designed and built guided missile frigate, and the diplomacy that could be achieved through the shared language of the open sea. As the journey neared its end, Vishal counted the days until he could hold Payal in his arms again. The frigate returned to Indian shores, greeted by the cheers and applause of those who recognized the significance of its mission.

Payal waited yet another month for Vishal to come back home in Delhi, her eyes searching for Vishal's familiar face. The reunion was emotional and joyous. Vishal and Payal embraced, cherishing the moment that marked the end of their physical separation. The sacrifices made for duty had only strengthened their love, and they both knew that their journey, individually and as a couple, had been extraordinary. Both, united once more, looked towards the future with a shared sense of pride and commitment. Their love had withstood the challenges of a long and demanding journey, proving that even oceans apart, the bond they shared was unbreakable. Now for the first time, Payal would be leaving home at Delhi to join the Vishal in Bombay and start their family journey together, unaware that fate would bring them both back soon to Delhi.

Navigating the Depths: A Naval Architect's Odyssey

Within six months since the Godavari had returned from the global tour, Vishal found himself posted to the Naval Headquarters, New Delhi. A quiet experienced ship constructor and naval architect by now, he was part of a project that would test the limits of engineering prowess of the entire project team. Having spent years at sea, hands-on with operational vessels, he now stood at the forefront of a unique national mission – part of an esteemed team that is mandated to design a nuclear-powered submarine for Indian Navy. Project of submarine design worked under overall charge of Director General Naval Design.

The submarine project was shrouded in secrecy and complexity. Vishal worked with a team, many superior to him and specialised in submarine technology, and were brilliant engineers, naval architects, and physicists, each contributing their expertise to the intricate puzzle that was nuclear submarine design. The challenges were immense, from ensuring the vessel's hull with stealth capabilities to optimizing the nuclear propulsion system for maximum efficiency.

The initial project team included select members who either had experienced Indian submarine construction at Germany and were overseeing its construction at HDW Shipyard, Germany or were part of its technical commissioning crew. The project team was expanded slowly as it progressed and new members started to join in and so was Vishal. Commodore Roy, a seasoned Naval Architect had assumed the role of its Director. He, and his team of three top Joint Directors were all part of the team those who had got experience at Germany. So were the three shipwright artificers Kumar, Rathore and Bajwa whom Vishal had joined, all senior to him.

As the project progressed, team faced many herculin task in way, grappling with the nuances of submarine design. The weight of responsibility rested on their shoulders, and they realised the gravity of the task at hand. The successful execution of the project could redefine the capabilities of the navy, and failure was not an option. The challenges were unprecedented. The intricacies of nuclear propulsion demanded a level of precision that left no room for error. Nuclear power reactor, Pressure hull design, Hydrodynamics, Propulsion system, Stealth technology, Weapon launch and safety protocols required meticulous attention. Yet, team of naval engineers along with many civilian design officers and draftsman working in the office embraced the complexity, finding inspiration in the unknown depths that lay beneath the ocean's surface.

The large hall donned many big sized drawing boards, with draftsman, design officers and engineers leaning on there. Occasionally, going through drawing in microfilm projection system for references. Vishal and other shipwright engineers had the responsibility of converting design drawings into an accurate scale model of the submarine, built in transparent acrylic and colour pipes and wires. The physical model of submarine displayed all installed machineries, complex network of piping, electrical systems, power reactors and other equipment for feasibility checks in a space constrained area. This is substituted today by three-dimensional computer modelling with software program like Tribon or Catia. Physical modelling was based on technology acquired from Ingenteur Kontor, Lubeck in West Germany.

The Naval Headquarters buzzed with anticipation as the design phase progressed. Project Director regularly presented their ongoing progress to high-ranking officials, such as Scientific advisor to Government, Director General Naval Design, Vice Chief of Naval Staff and Controller of Warship Production. The intricate dance of charts, graphs, microfilms, and technical jargon painted a vivid picture of the potential of this groundbreaking vessel. Design office was frequented by top level officials concerned with project, to witness the submarine model for better appreciation. All who had seen the blueprint of progress made and how things are planned for next few years, gave a sense that day is not far when nation would be witnessing the launch of our very own nuclear-powered submarine.

Life in the Home City

Vishal and Payal have returned to Delhi within six months since they together moved to Bombay. Vishal had found himself embedded in a high-strategic navy project of utmost secrecy. The nature of his work required him to tiptoe around the inquisitive inquiries of his wife, Payal, about the specifics of his day-to-day tasks. Every evening, Vishal would return home to Payal, who brimmed with curiosity about his work. However, the classified nature of his project meant he had to master the art of evasion and employ vague responses to sidestep her probing questions.

Vishal's commute, a daily venture through the polluted air and smoke of the Delhi's ring road, offered him moments of anxiety as he navigated his Vespa scooter through the bustling traffic. The 20 km journey from West Delhi to his office in South Delhi provided Vishal with a blend of challenges and reflections. The hum of the scooter's engine intertwined with the city's cacophony as he maneuverer through the crowded roads. The pollution seemed to thicken the air, creating a protective shroud that mirrored the secrecy he maintained about his work.

Payal, an understanding and supportive wife, couldn't help but wonder about the enigma that was Vishal's professional life. "How was your day?" she'd inquire with a sparkle in her eyes, eager for a glimpse into his world. Vishal, in turn, became a master of ambiguity, weaving tales of generic office happenings and bureaucratic procedures. As the days turned into weeks, Vishal's routine of evading Payal's innocent inquiries became second nature. Yet, he couldn't help but marvel at the resilience of their relationship, grounded in trust despite the unspoken boundaries surrounding his work.

Payal, understanding the unspoken dynamics, always returned the smile, recognizing the unspoken commitment they shared. In that moment, amidst the chaos of a bustling city and the veil of secrecy surrounding Vishal's work, the couple found solace in the bond they had built—a bond that withstood the challenges of secrecy and thrived in the unspoken understanding that defined their relationship. One fine evening, Vishal had just returned home from another gruelling day at the Naval Design Bureau in Delhi. The weather outside had been hot and relentless, and the long hours spent at work poring over blueprints and documents had left him exhausted. As he walked through the door of his modest apartment, the cool air and familiar scent of home instantly soothed him.

"Payal, I'm home!" he called out. From the kitchen, Payal emerged, her face lighting up with a warm smile. You look tired. How was your day?"

Vishal sighed, running a hand through his hair. "Hectic, as usual. Payal's eyes sparkled with a hint of mischief. "Well, I have something that might just make your evening even better."

Curiosity piqued; Vishal raised an eyebrow. "Oh? What's that?"

"Sit down," Payal instructed gently, leading him to the living room sofa. As Vishal settled into the cushions, she sat beside him, taking his hand in hers.

"Vishal, there's something I've been wanting to tell you, she began, her voice trembling slightly with emotion. Vishal's heart skipped a beat. "What is it, Payal? You're starting to worry me."

Payal took a deep breath, her eyes locking onto his. "I'm pregnant, Vishal. We're going to have a baby."

For a moment, the world around Vishal seemed to blur. He stared at Payal, his mind racing to catch up with the enormity of her words.

"We're… going to have a baby?" he repeated, his voice barely above a whisper.

Payal nodded, her eyes glistening with tears of joy. "Yes, we are. I found out a few days ago. I wanted to tell you sooner, but I wanted to make sure everything was okay first."

A flood of emotions washed over Vishal—joy, excitement, and a profound sense of wonder. He felt a lump form in his throat as he pulled Payal into a tight embrace. "This is… this is incredible, Payal. I can't believe it. We're going to be parents!"

As they held each other, Vishal's mind raced with thoughts of the future. He imagined their child growing up, the laughter and the milestones, the challenges and the triumphs. The long hours at the office suddenly seemed insignificant compared to the life-changing news Payal had just shared.

"I'm so happy," he murmured into her hair. "So incredibly happy. How are you feeling? Are you okay?"

Payal pulled back slightly, smiling through her tears. "I'm feeling good, just a little tired and nauseous at times. But it's all worth it." Vishal nodded; his expression serious but tender. "We'll take this journey together. I'll be here for you every step of the way."

They spent the rest of the evening talking about their hopes and dreams for their future family. Payal shared her plans and the books she had been reading, while Vishal marvelled at the idea of fatherhood. The weight of the day's work lifted from his shoulders, replaced by a new sense of purpose and excitement.

That night, as Vishal lay beside his wife, he felt a deep sense of contentment. The road ahead would undoubtedly be filled with challenges, but with Payal by his side and a baby on the way, he knew that their love and resilience would carry them through. And for the first time in a long while, Vishal fell asleep with a smile on his face, dreaming of the beautiful journey that awaited them.

Turbulence in the Family- Transfer Move

Into the fifth year of Vishal posting at Delhi, they had by now moved to their own new house in Gurgaon. Payal stood by the window, gazing out at the familiar skyline. The city, which had been her home for years, suddenly felt like an echo of the life she knew. Her husband, Vishal, a Master Chief Shipwright Artificer now, had just received news of his posting to the distant shores of Port Blair. With a three-year-old daughter Monisha clinging to her side, the news hit Payal like a tidal wave of emotions.

As she processed the reality of the impending move, Payal's heart swirled with a mix of conflicting feelings. Port Blair, a picturesque island in the Andaman and Nicobar archipelago, held promises of new adventures, but it also meant leaving behind the comfort and familiarity of around Delhi, where their roots were deeply embedded. Vishal, bound by duty to his naval career, tried to ease Payal's concerns, assuring her that this was a part of the journey they had chosen together. But Payal couldn't shake the bittersweet taste of farewell that lingered in the air.

The thought of uprooting their lives, with a little one in tow, weighed heavily on Payal's heart. She couldn't help but feel a pang of sadness for the friendships they would leave behind, the bustling Delhi streets that echoed with memories, and the family gatherings that would become distant echoes. As the days passed, Payal found solace in the support of her family and friends, who gathered around her, helping pack up their home and offering words of encouragement. The little daughter, sensing the change, clung to her mother a little tighter, as if intuitively understanding that a significant shift was on the horizon.

As they were preparing for the move, Vishal and Payal received news that filled their hearts with both excitement and trepidation – Payal was pregnant once again. Amidst the joy of expanding their family, they were faced with the reality of Vishal's impending posting to Port Blair. With mixed emotions, they embraced the changes that lay ahead, determined to navigate this new chapter of their lives with courage and grace. In the chaos of packing, Payal took moments to reflect on the love story she and Vishal had written together first in Delhi and now living at their own home in Gurgaon. The milestones they had celebrated, the challenges they had overcome, and the dreams they had woven into the fabric of their home suddenly felt like fragile threads, vulnerable to the winds of change.

As the time to move to Port Blair drew near, Vishal and Payal bid farewell to the city of Delhi and Gurgaon, where they had celebrated Monisha's growing up surrounded by friends and family. Payal, now two months pregnant, held Monisha's hand tightly as they boarded the train for Chennai for onward flight to Port Blair. They arrived in Chennai and prepared to ship their belongings and LML Vespa scooter by ship to Port Blair. In the late evening all three celebrated Monisha's third birthday in the hotel they stayed in. Next day morning they were to take flight for Port Blair.

A New Beginning - Alas Heavenly

It was first plane journey for Payal and Monisha both. Excited as she was, Monisha was looking out from plane window, exclaimed seeing vast sea below. Port Blair, with its azure waters and lush landscapes, welcoming the family, offering the promise of new beginnings. And as Payal looked out at the ocean stretching before her, she realized that the love and resilience that had sustained them in Delhi would be the guiding stars in this new chapter of their lives. Vishal was struck by the natural beauty that surrounded him. Lush greenery, pristine beaches, and the azure waters of the Bay of Bengal greeted them.

Vishal took his posting to Port Blair with mixed feelings. Leaving behind the streets of Delhi and Gurgaon, he was both excited and apprehensive about the prospect of life on a distant island in the Andaman Sea. Little did he know that his senior colleague, Kushal had already orchestrated a warm welcome and a seamless transition for him and his family. As Vishal, Monisha and Payal, stepped off the plane in Port Blair, the tropical breeze greeted them. But what awaited them was more than just the beauty of the island; it was the warmth of friendship and the support of a naval family. Kushal was at the airport to welcome them. Kushal was four-year senior to Vishal and by now has seasoned presence on the island and workplace, had made meticulous arrangements. A cozy house awaited them, and ready to become their new home. The thoughtful gesture touched Vishal and Payal, providing a sense of comfort in this unfamiliar environment. From running around for gas connection to other essential, Kushal made sure Vishal and Payal are not inconvenienced.

As the family settled into their new home in Port Blair, Payal held onto the memories of Delhi like cherished treasures. With each passing day, the island embraced them with its own unique charm, and Payal found herself slowly learning to call it home. Through the laughter of her daughter and the anticipation of a new addition to their family, Payal discovered that love could indeed transcend the boundaries of time and space, creating a home wherever the heart may be.

Payal found Leela, Kushal's wife, a friend to rely on for any help in early days of their settlement. Monisha found a friend in Kushal's daughter Mili. They would often play together now, and Monisha slowly made more friends as she joined a new school. As Payal's pregnancy progressed, Vishal made sure to prioritize her well-being and comfort, accompanying her to doctor's appointments and ensuring she received the best possible care. Monisha, excited to become a big sister, showered her mother with love and affection, eagerly anticipating the arrival of her new sibling. Despite the distance from their family, Vishal and Payal found support and camaraderie in their new community in Port Blair. Leela was always there to support. They forged friendships with fellow naval families, who welcomed them with open arms and shared in their excitement for the impending arrival of their newest family member.

As Payal's due date approached, Vishal and Payal felt a mixture of nerves and anticipation, eager to meet their newest addition. In the quiet moments between duty and preparation, they cherished the precious time they spent together as a family, savouring the simple joys of togetherness and love. Finally, the long-awaited day arrived, and Payal was admitted to hospital INHS Dhanvantri at Minnie Bay and gave birth to another beautiful baby girl, completing their family in a burst of joy and love. As they cradled their newborn in their arms, Vishal and Payal felt an overwhelming sense of gratitude and wonder, marvelling at the miracle of life and the blessings that surrounded them.

In the days and weeks that followed, Vishal and Payal settled into their roles as parents of two, embracing the challenges and joys that came with raising a growing family. With Monisha doting on her baby sister and Payal embracing her new role as a mother of two, their home was filled with laughter, love, and the sweet sounds of childhood. As they looked back on their journey, Vishal and Payal knew that they had faced many challenges and sacrifices along the way, but they also knew that every moment had been worth it to see the smiles on their children's faces and feel the warmth of their love. Together, they embraced the adventure of parenthood, knowing that their bond as a family would carry them through whatever life had in store.

Surprise Gurgaon Connection.

Amidst the chaos of work at floating dock floor, another marine engineer Suresh, one of the Engine Room Artificer in floating dry dock, diligently carried out his duties. He was a young man with a heart as vast as the ocean itself, and his dedication to his work was matched only by his kindness towards his fellow crew.

One sunny morning, a in the busy floor of the dry dock, Vishal, as newcomer who had just arrived at Port Blair met Suresh. Vishal was bit lost in the sea of unfamiliar faces and routines. Sensing Vishal's unease, Suresh extended a friendly hand and introduced himself and explained functioning of dock. Suresh was four years junior to Vishal in Navy. During discussion and informal introduction, what surprisingly emerged common was Gurgaon connection to which they both belonged, Suresh by virtue of ancestral and while Vishal by settlement.

From explaining the inner workings of the floating dry dock to introducing to the best places to grab a bite to eat on shore leave, Suresh was there every step of the way. Vishal stayed on the same building in Minie Bay area as Suresh and this led to closer family bonding. As time went on, Suresh and Vishal's bond grew stronger, transcending the boundaries of mere friendship to become more like family. Suresh became a constant presence in Vishal's life, at Port Blair offering support, and a listening ear whenever needed. Suresh and his wife Kavita were always a call away whenever needed and stood by them throughout particularly during Payal's pregnancy.

An Island made of Steel- Floating Dry Dock

Vishal found himself a new mission: to man a Floating Dry Dock, part of the Naval Ship Repair Yard at Port Blair and oversee docking, undocking, the repair, and maintenance of naval ships in the idyllic but challenging waters surrounding the archipelago. A seasoned Master Chief

Shipwright Artificer, and hull engineer, thrived in the dynamic world of naval maintenance at the bustling dry dock.

A conventional graving dock is a land based concrete structure with Cashion gate at one end towards sea. The opening of Cashion gate allows sea water to flood the dock up to outside sea level and ship to enters inside. Dock gates are then closed watertight and inside water is completely pumped out slowly to allow ship to sit on the dock blocks at pre-determined position.

Unlike a conventional graving dock, A floating dry dock is a remarkable engineering steel structure that serves as a versatile platform for the repair, maintenance, and construction of ships and vessels. It can be moored at a jetty for operation or positioned away from shore in deep sea water moored permanently with anchors. It is a U-shaped steel structure where two vertical sides of U are side wing structure housing machineries, Cranes, workshop, Control Room, limited accommodation and partly water tanks. While the bottom horizontal of U is a box like structure containing ballast tanks and Pump Rooms, where top surface of tanks serve as dock floors to position the ships.

Floating Dry Dock Moored at Port Blair Harbour

Built in Japan by Ishikawajima-Harima Heavy Industries, the floating dry dock was 188 meter long, 40-meter-wide, and 15-meter-deep Caisson type steel structure with a total lifting capacity of 11500 metric tonnes ship. It had total 24 numbers of double bottom water ballast tanks of which 12 tanks were L shaped tank including some part of wings as tanks. These tanks are used for ballasting/ De-ballasting of water and for controlled submergence and structural deflection like hogging and sagging moment of the dock, and for controlling list, and trim during docking and undocking operation.

Once the floating dry dock is submerged by ballasting of tanks to required level based on ship's draft, the ship to be serviced enters through the open side end. After the ship is positioned correctly within the dry dock, the ballast tanks are emptied of water, causing the dock to rise and lift the ship along completely above out of the water. As the floating dry dock rises, the ship is evenly supported by a series of side blocks and centre keel blocks, strategically placed on the dock floor. These blocks provide stability and support for the ship's hull, ensuring that it remains secure and stable during the servicing process.

Moment the ship is lifted out of the water, engineer, technicians, and workers have access to the underwater hull for inspection, cleaning, maintenance, and repair. This includes tasks such as painting, welding, hull cleaning, anode renewal, propellers and rudders maintenance, valves replacement, Sonar, Speed Log and Echo Sounder sensors checks and repair, and for any structural repairs required. On completion of work, the ship is lowered back into the water by refilling the ballast tanks with water. This causes the floating dry dock to descend, allowing the ship float back and exit through the one end.

Throughout the entire process, safety is paramount, with strict protocols and procedures in place to ensure the smooth and efficient operation of the floating dry dock. From the initial submersion to the final de submersion, each step is carefully conducted to ensure the successful servicing of ships and vessels of all sizes.

Island Odyssey: A Naval Engineer's Voyage

Kushal, being the experienced hand, took Vishal under his wing, introducing him to the intricacies of their work in the Floating Dry Dock. The two worked side by side for one year, exchanging insights and experiences, forming a professional bond that transcended the workplace. He was quickly learning all the intricacy of floating dry dock.

As part of preparation before a naval vessel approached floating dry dock for docking, Vishal and his team would meticulously arrange the dock blocks on the dock floor surface every time. The placement of these blocks was akin to a well-choreographed dance between cranes and concrete block, with each block shaped to ships bottom profile placed at its resting position.

The docking plan, a blueprint of precision, guided Vishal's decisions on the optimal positioning of the vessel within the dry dock. The success of the operation depended on aligning the ship with the carefully placed dock blocks, ensuring that the vessel's weight was adequately distributed among the number of blocks and that critical areas requiring maintenance were accessible.

At times dock undertook multiple docking of up to three ships simultaneously, and this was an intricate and complex operation which Vishal mastered under mentorship with likes of Kushal and others in due course of time.

Operation Docking- A Masterpiece of Coordination

In the Floating Dry Dock, Vishal, had completed one year by now and was leading the team as Master Chief Shipwright, orchestrated a ballet of precision and expertise as he ensured the seamless docking or undocking of a vessel. The rhythmic sound of machinery, the occasional clang of metal, and a windy salty breeze set the stage for a process that required meticulous planning and flawless execution.

Vishal often found himself at the helm of operation on the floating dry dock. He was ably assisted by his junior shipwright artificer Atul Kumar, Sunil Joshi, Om, Shamsher and others. The task at hand was to smoothly position naval vessel within the dock, ensuring that every element of the process unfolded with meticulous accuracy. He would discuss the plan in detail with dock master and shipwright officer every time a ship is planned to be docked or undocked and go about his responsibilities to execute. Vishal's responsibilities included overseeing the repair on the floating dry dock. Each vessel that arrived for maintenance or repairs brought with it a unique set of challenges, requiring a tailored approach to the docking process.

Every time a vessel approached for docking; Vishal's team will swiftly take control of the floating dock's winches fitted on four top corners of the floating dock. The winches were crucial in controlling the movement of the vessel as it navigated into the floating dock. Each winch wire was meticulously attached to the ship, ready to be operated with precision. A crucial component of this operation was the traveling block – a mechanism that moved along guided rails on the floating dock. The traveling block was connected to the ship through a system of wire ropes and pulleys, creating a controlled connection for hauling the vessel into the dock.

With the vessel hovering at the entrance of the floating dock, Vishal oversees entry of vessel into the dock, his team start the controlled manoeuvring while maintaining communication on walkie talkie with each position. The winches begin to tighten, pulling the ship with calculated force. The traveling blocks smoothly glides along the rails, ensuring a controlled and guided entry of the vessel into the dock in synchronised way, and finally position the vessel as planned. The positioning of the vessel's keel aligning with the centre of dock blocks required meticulous coordination. Vishal, relying on his years of experience and expertise, maintaining communication with the dock operators and crew members to ensure that the vessel settled precisely onto the blocks. Once ship reached the marked position, centreline of the ship had to be horizontally aligned with the help of plumb line at both forward and aft end, with centre line of floating dock. It is a delicate balance, a moment where the combined forces of wind, gravity and engineering must be in harmony.

Vishal, standing at a vantage point, centre of fly bridge at extreme forward, directed the operation with precision. His experience and expertise were evident as the vessel inched closer, aligning perfectly with the dock blocks while the dockmaster, a shipwright or construction officer, frequenting in between the control room and outside deck monitoring and managing ballasting and ship's movement. The synchronized efforts of the winches, traveling block, and the floating dock's de-ballasting process ensured a seamless positioning of the vessel inside the dry dock.

As soon as vessel reaches its pre-determined position, dock master starts ascent of floating dry dock by de-ballasting. The tanks, once filled with water, began to release their cargo, causing the dock to rise gradually. This synchronized dance between the winches, the traveling block, and the de-ballasting of the dock required flawless coordination. Once the vessel was securely in place, Vishal oversaw the final stages of the docking process. The dock continued to rise until the vessel's keel was comfortably cradled on the dock blocks, signalling the successful completion of this intricate operation.

As the floating dry dock completed its ascent and dock floor rises above water, Vishal and his team go down to dock floor for initial inspection to plan and prepare the vessel for maintenance and repair activity. The entire operation, orchestrated with precision and expertise, showcased Vishal's and team's commitment to excellence in naval repair and his ability to navigate complex processes with finesse.

An Action-packed Workstation- Dock Floor

On a next bright morning, Vishal stood on the floating dry dock floor, a colossal platform for ships maintenance. With the initial survey completed, the dock buzzed with activity as team sprang into action and cleaned entire ship hull with hydro jetting, removing all fouling and marine growth to the maximum extent, exposing its hull to the elements. Vishal instructed to start blasting process once hull is cleaned and dry, where high-pressure abrasive material like coarse sand, steel shot or copper slag are used to remove old paint, rust, and any existing corrosion. The deafening roar of the blasting machines echoed through the dock as the hull was slowly stripped down to bare metal steel grade SA 2.5 and one coat of primer paint applied immediately on bare metal surface for protection.

Underwater hull survey is then undertaken for sign of deteriorated hull plates and marked for renewal where necessary as first step in the process of hull inspection. Vishal and his team, armed with specialized tools and equipment, carefully inspected every nook and cranny of the ship's hull. They document any signs of corrosion, damage, or wear and tear that needed attention. This comprehensive survey formed the blueprint for the upcoming maintenance work.

As the lead engineer overseeing hull protection, he meticulously planned and executed the essential tasks that would shield the ship's underbelly from the harsh elements of the sea. His expertise lay in the intricate details of ship hull protection – a critical aspect that ensured the longevity and efficiency of naval vessels. Once the hull was cleaned, Impressed Cathodic Protection system examined and FRP shielding repaired all around. The sacrificial anodes replaced where perished above fifty percent.

A team of engineers work on to inspect the Shafting, Propellers, and Rudder for sign of defect or any damage. One by one each part was dismantled and lowered on the dock floor protected from any dust or contamination. Preparation started to thoroughly examine, note clearances, and see for pitting marks or potential damage on the rudder and propellers shafts. The shaft bearings, seals and bushes replaced where needed.

Underwater valves and other hull valves were removed for servicing. Anchor Chain Cables lowered on dock floor for survey and conditioning. Every activity needed to be attended during dry docking was systematically attended to complete. Electrical engineers would check and overhaul the sensors of echo sounder, speed log and sonar.

Vishal led the team and embarked on the meticulous process of protective coats application. The first layer of primer paint, a corrosion-resistant base that would ensure the subsequent layers adhered securely is followed by two coats of anti-corrosive coating, a specialized barrier that shielded the hull from the corrosive effects of saltwater, are applied. The final three coats of anti-fouling painting, a high-quality anti-fouling epoxy paint designed to prevent the marine growth and organisms on the ship's hull are then applied. This not only preserved the ship's performance but also reduced fuel consumption by maintaining a smooth and clean surface.

As Vishal oversaw the painting process; he couldn't help but marvel at the transformation unfolding before him. The once-fouled hull, thick with sea weeds and hard sea barnacles, now gleamed with multiple layers of protective coatings, ready to brave the open sea once again. The meticulous attention to detail paid off as the ship, now cocooned in its protective layers, was gently floated back into the water.

As the ship sailed away from the floating dry dock, Vishal and team watched with pride, knowing that his team had played a crucial role in ensuring the vessel's seaworthiness so as other engineers who ensured that everything was taken care to the best. The hull, fortified against the challenges of the sea, was a testament to the skill and commitment of the artificer's engineers who laboured tirelessly to protect the backbone of the naval fleet.

INS Yamuna-A Challenging Task

A survey ship INS Yamuna was arriving from Kochi to Port Blair for the planned docking next on floating dry dock. Ship was coming for complete change of its underwater paint scheme. With a reputation for meticulous planning and an expertise in ship maintenance, Vishal knew that responsibility lay ahead.

The ship, a survey vessel of the Indian Navy, sailed into the dry dock with a purpose. Vishal's mind buzzed with the intricacies of the task at hand as he planned for the complete hull survey. The dry dock, a floating platform with a purpose, eagerly awaited its next occupant. Vishal, armed with blueprints and an acute understanding of the ship's structure, strategized the docking arrangements. As ship docked inside on the decided day, multiple activities sprang into action.

Every detail, from the hull survey to mechanical maintenance, was carefully mapped out to ensure a seamless operation. The hull survey involved a comprehensive examination of every inch beneath the waterline. Vishal's team of skilled inspectors scoured the hull for signs of wear, corrosion, and damage. The clock ticked relentlessly, and Vishal knew that time was of the essence.

Floating dock had recently received two new Vacuum Blasting machines for hull preparation and to mitigate environmental concern. These machines provided safe and efficient operation though much slower compared to open shot blasting which were planned to be phased out. With these machines all dust and debris are collected at the blasting gun point itself, preventing debris from flying into the air or sea. Once the work commenced, teams to their horror find old paint on ship's hull intact rock solid. Vacuum blasting machines roared to life, removing layers of old paint and rust from the ship's surface. A team of workers would every day go about the process and until entire old paint was removed to bare hull and primed. Vishal supervised the entire application of fresh coatings, a crucial step in preserving the hull's integrity and ensuring longevity. The seven layers of paint consisting of Primer, Anti corrosive and Anti fouling paints had to be applied on entire underwater hull, totalling to 700–800-micron thickness.

Underwater, mechanical maintenance tasks unfolded like a symphony of precision. Shafts, propellers, and rudders underwent thorough examinations and necessary repairs. Hull anodes were replaced, and the Impressed Current Cathodic. The hull mounted sensors of Echo Sounder and Speed Log were examined and serviced. All essential checks required during docking are completed one by one. The INS Yamuna, once a vessel in need of care, emerged from the dry dock with a rejuvenated hull and enhanced mechanical systems. Vishal's meticulous planning had not only met but exceeded expectations. The success of the docking operation was a testament to floating dock crew's expertise.

The Unfortunate Docking- Mishap in the Making

In the bustling floating dry dock at Port Blair, the routine of maritime operations hummed like a well-oiled machine. Ships came and went, and among the essential facilities at the floating dock, that provided maintenance and repair services to vessels of all sizes. On a particularly sunny morning, the tranquil waters of the port bore witness to a docking operation that would soon veer off course. Voices from naval ship INS Prahar boomed over the radio broadcast as ship approached floating dry dock. The tug master assisting ship for the cold move were in constant communication with the dock master. It was due for routine maintenance, and the crew eagerly anticipated a swift turnaround.

Meanwhile, on the floating dry dock, Master Chief Shipwright Artificer Vishal had double-checked the docking arrangement as per the plans provided by the ship. The dock block arrangement was executed by team led by Shipwright Artificer Third Engineer Atul Kumar in line with the docking plan. As the ship neared the floating dry dock, excitement mingled with tension in the air. The crew on both sides prepared for the intricate ballet of manoeuvring the massive vessel into place. However, it soon became apparent that something was off. The ship didn't settle into place as expected, and the tension in the air thickened with each passing moment.

With mounting dread, Vishal and Dock Master realized the gravity of the situation and became aware of the consequences. The misaligned dock blocks were causing the ship to list dangerously to one side. Panic rippled through the ship's crew as they scrambled to salvage the situation, but time was slipping away, and the situation grew increasingly precarious.

In the Wheelhouse of the ship, Captain shouted orders, his voice strained with urgency. The floating dock was in de-ballasting mode and docking team needed to stabilize and control the ship before it capsized entirely. With nerves of steel, Vishal coordinated a desperate effort and informed dock master of the critical situation who immediately ordered ballasting of the floating dock at full speed to free float the ship once again, battling against the force of gravity. The control room came in swift mode and reversed the operation. Once ship was afloat, it was immediately pulled out of the dock and taken to the berth until next plan of action is in place. A sigh of relief perpetuated all around on averting of catastrophic situation.

The entire technical team headed by dock master gathered in the briefing room with drawings and plans in hand to deliberated cause of this mishappening. The command headquarter was informed of situation who in turn started investigation at their end. The Chief Staff Officer (Technical) assisted by his team of officers from Command Headquarter too joined in the deliberation at floating dock. The docking plan with dock blocks laid on the floor was reconciled, and they were found in order as per the plan.

As investigation progressed at different level, at around midnight, it was let known to the floating dock that probably a wrong plan has been shared with the dock. Due to this miscommunication between the ship's crew and the office, the dimensions and placement of the dock blocks were incorrect. In the aftermath of the near-disaster, an exhaustive investigation confirmed the source of the mishap—the erroneous docking plans was provided by the ship. How it happened was a matter to be investigated later by authority. Lessons were learned, and protocols were tightened to prevent such a debacle from ever happening again. As for the ship INS Prahar and the floating dock authorities, their swift thinking and decisive action saved the day, earning them the admiration and gratitude of their respective crews. Minutes stretched into an eternity as the fate of "Prahar" hung in the balance.

By next day morning, the correct docking plan was shared with the floating dock. The dock block arrangement was modified to the new plan and checked and rechecked for assurance before the go ahead was given. Two days later, with another attempt and collective gasp, the ship successfully shifted into alignment, its hull settling snugly into the cradle of the floating dry dock. Cheers erupted from both sides as relief washed over them like a tidal wave.

The tale of the misguided docking would become a cautionary legend whispered among maritime circles, a reminder of the unforgiving nature of the sea and the importance of precision in every aspect of seafaring life.

A Slight Negligence- Mishap in the Waiting

In the floating dock, a colossal structure that housed the mightiest naval vessels, alongside Vishal it was Sameer's workplace as well where he, as Master Chief Electrical Artificer, spent his days ensuring the seamless functioning of the ship's electrical power systems. Little did he know that one fateful event would test his mettle in a way he had never imagined. One routine day, Sameer and his team were on a task to resolve a technical glitch on deck crane of the dry dock. The massive crane, essential for the maintenance of the ships, had encountered some electrical issue that needed immediate attention. Sameer along with his team of engineers, armed with tools and expertise, climbed onto the crane's structure, determined to diagnose, and fix the problem. As Sameer delved into the intricate wiring and components, his focus was unwavering. He meticulously traced the electrical circuits, searching for the root cause of the malfunction.

However, during his troubleshooting, an unforeseen mishap occurred. The deck crane, with blaring horn, started to move along its track, catching Sameer in its mechanical grip. Panic surged through Sameer as the massive crane began to close the distance between him and the railing of the floating dry dock. The situation turned dire as he found himself trapped between the unyielding railing and the moving crane body. The realization of the imminent danger sent shivers down his spine. His team, witnessing the unfolding disaster, reacted swiftly. Amid the chaos, one of Sameer's vigilant team members, quick to assess the severity of the situation, rushed to the emergency switch. With a decisive flick, he shut down the power supply to the deck crane, bringing it to a sudden halt. The deafening silence that followed was broken only by the collective sighs of relief from Sameer's teammates. The potential catastrophe had been averted, thanks to the presence of mind and quick actions of his fellow engineers.

As the dust settled, it became apparent that Sameer, though narrowly escaping a tragedy, had sustained injuries. With a broken hand and serious bruises, he was quickly and carefully extricated from the confined space. The urgency of the situation prompted his teammates to rush him to the hospital for immediate medical attention. The incident served as a stark reminder of the risks inherent in the realm of heavy machinery and complex systems. Sameer's resilience and his team's swift response not only prevented a catastrophic event but also underscored the importance of teamwork and preparedness in the face of unforeseen challenges. The floating dry dock, witness to both the potential dangers and the triumph of human ingenuity, continued its duty, a silent sentinel on the waters, as Sameer embarked on the path to recovery.

Goodbye to The Paradise

Life on the Andaman Islands brought unique challenges. The isolation demanded self-sufficiency, as supplies arrived sporadically. Vishal had adapted, turning the challenges into opportunities to showcase their resourcefulness. But it wasn't just the technical aspects that made Vishal's journey memorable; it was the bond he formed with the islanders. The vibrant local culture, a fusion of indigenous traditions and naval camaraderie, became an integral part of his experience. The islanders, with their warm hospitality, embraced the naval presence, forming a symbiotic relationship that transcended the professional realm. As the years passed, Vishal witnessed the transformation of the Andaman Islands and the floating dry dock's role in enhancing naval capabilities in the region. His tenure on this remote outpost became a chapter in his naval career that was as fulfilling as it was challenging.

Fourteen years had gone by since completion of his training, and Vishal, once a fresh-faced engineer, now stood as a seasoned veteran of the sea. His journey to the Andaman Islands had not only tested his technical acumen but had also enriched his understanding of naval engineering and operations and strengthened his bond with the ocean.

As Vishal prepared for his next posting, he left the Andaman Islands with a heart full of memories and a legacy of maritime excellence. His journey, shaped by the rhythm of the sea and the resilience of naval personnel, was a testament to the unyielding spirit that defined the navy's commitment to safeguarding the seas.

Waves of Reflection- The Final Voyage

Vishal, with a career spanning eighteen years since he had joined for naval training as a young seventeen-year boy, now stood on the deck of the INS Sutlej, the ocean survey ship that would be his final posting before he sailed into civilian life. The ship's hull gleamed white in the sunlight as it bobbed gently in the Cochin harbour, ready to chart the unexplored depths of the ocean.

The INS Sutlej set sail frequently for hydrographic survey of sea, a task for which ship was designed, with an expert hydrographer Captain at helm, along with and many other crew members specialised in the task of hydrographic survey. As the ship ventured into the open sea, Vishal couldn't escape the waves of reflection that washed over him.

The rhythmic hum of the engines and machineries, sound of horn, running of capstan & windlasses, boat davits, hoisting of anchor chain cables at forecastle and the salty breeze hitting against his face, and the vast expanse of the ocean mirrored the journey of his naval career. The survey boats and davit system of ship was prime focus of Vishal as these were the lifeline serving team of crew who would venture out on boat to sea with survey equipment or proceed to shore to set up hydrography survey base units. Over the next year, Vishal watched other expert crew in sea through the intricacies of hydrographic surveying. The ship became a floating laboratory, equipped with state-of-the-art technology to map the ocean floor, update sea navigational chart, and explore its mysteries.

As the days turned into weeks, Vishal found solace in the routine of ship life. He shared stories with his crew, passing on the wisdom accumulated over nearly two decades of naval service. Together, they faced the challenges of the open sea, from unpredictable weather to technical malfunctions, with a camaraderie forged through shared experiences. But beneath the surface of routine, there lingered a sense of finality. Vishal knew that this would be his last voyage on a naval ship.

The time had come to transition to a new chapter in his life, one that would take him from the uniformed world to the civilian realm. After INS Sutlej returned to port one last time before its time for Vishal to pack his baggage, he felt a bittersweet mix of emotions. The ship's hull creaked gently against the dock, a sound that echoed the closing of one chapter and the opening of another. He looked out at the vast expanse of the sea, knowing that this would be the last time he stood on the deck as a naval artificer. With a salute to the ship that had been his companion for the past year, Vishal stepped onto solid ground, ready to face the challenges of civilian life. His naval career had been a journey of dedication and service, but the time had come to set a new course and embrace the uncharted waters of the civilian world.

As Vishal hung up his naval uniform, he carried with him the memories of the sea, the friendships forged in the crucible of naval service, and the lessons learned from nearly two decades of sailing beneath the Indian flag. And with a heart full of gratitude and anticipation, he set forth on the next challenging career that awaited him in the civilian realm, ready to make waves of a different kind.

PART 3

ABOUT NAVAL ARTIFICER

Beyond the Waves: Charting of New Horizons

In the naval fraternity, where camaraderie thrived and bonds were forged amidst the noise and vibration of machinery and the salt-laden breeze, a unique trend persisted among the esteemed Naval Artificer Engineers. These skilled engineers, after reaching the height of their naval career in short time while still young, find themselves at a crossroads where they could choose to explore opportunities beyond the uniform. While the path to commissioned officer is an option, significant number of naval artificers opt for an alternative journey, one that lead them beyond the confines of naval life and into the vast expanse of the civilian world.

An Artificer is described as a military engineer, a highly skilled craftsperson, one that contrives or constructs something. A specialised work force on a naval ship since the time of Royal Navy, artificers either worked as engine room engineers or electrical and electronics engineer or shipwright or an aviation artificer after they have successfully completed their four years training in their field before assigned to work on naval ships.

Among these enterprising individuals, the engine room artificers with their intricate knowledge of machinery systems, set sail for new horizons and find themselves navigating the merchant shipping, where their expertise in marine engines and propulsion is highly sought after and earns them hefty pay packages. The rhythmic heartbeat of engines resonated with their passion, and they embraced the challenges of the open seas in a different vessel, a vessel that bore the markings of commerce rather than war. Many go on to join the related industries in production or maintenance.

The electrical artificers, with their mastery over intricate electrical systems, face sea of opportunities. Some chose the allure of merchant navy vessels, where their skills were indispensable for ensuring the smooth operation of complex electrical networks. Others ventured into the civil world, where their expertise found applications in industries ranging from electronics and communications to power generation and distribution and many more such potentials.

Shipwright artificers, skilled in the art of ship construction and naval architecture, find their calling either in shipyards, heavy fabrication industry, marine surveying, or insurance underwritings. The echoes of their hammers and the caress of their skills resonate in shipyards both at home or abroad, where they contribute to the construction and maintenance of vessels across the globe. The shipyards became their new playground, and their expertise in crafting seafaring vessels became a sought-after commodity.

The aviation artificers move on to join as aircraft engineers with either airports, or private airlines or their service providers. Many move abroad to join likes of Boeing and Airbus, Lockheed Martin, Raytheon, and Northrop Grumman and while some work in their subsidiaries in India.

Interestingly, many naval artificers, irrespective of their trade, chose the path less travelled by starting their own business ventures. Drawing on the discipline and technical prowess homed in the navy, they carved out niches in various industries. From engineering workshops to consultancies to innovative technology startups, these former servicemen took the helm of their destinies and steered their businesses to remarkable success including on the global stage. The entrepreneurial odyssey of these naval artificers became a testament to their adaptability, resilience, and the profound impact of their naval training. Beyond the waves, in the vast sea of civilian opportunities, they showcased not only their technical prowess but also their ability to navigate uncharted territories and weather the storms of entrepreneurship.

Few have even explored the path of teaching in the technical institutes after acquiring higher qualifications and worked in institutes of prominence and have risen to Vice Chancellor as well.

As the naval uniform transformed into the attire of CEOs, captains of industry, and innovators, the legacy of these naval artificers continued to thrive. Their stories of success echoed in boardrooms, shipyards, and entrepreneurial circles, inspiring a new generation to embrace the limitless possibilities that awaited them beyond the familiar horizons of naval life.

Thousands of extraordinary professional journey by experienced artificers beyond their naval service like Vishal's, have run a successful course and each has a story to inspire other.

A Bond of Cherished Perseverance

Vishal's and Suresh had bonded well during their period at Port Blair while working together in Floating Dry Dock and this bond only grew stronger with time, transcending the period after Suresh left Port Blair. Years passed, and eventually, Suresh decided to bid farewell to his life in the navy. Vishal had also returned to Gurgaon on completion of service in Navy. On their return both have remained in touch throughout.

Suresh's journey was far from over. Returning to his hometown of Gurgaon, Suresh embarked on a new adventure - one that would see him carve out a path of success and achievement beyond his wildest dreams. Driven by his passion for engineering and a desire to give back to his community, Suresh founded chain of engineering colleges starting at Gurgaon. With a vision to provide quality education and empower the youth with the skills they needed to succeed, Suresh poured his heart and soul into his new venture. His way of giving back to society and shape his future post navy was quite unparalleled. The entire naval artificer community is proud of him.

Through hard work, perseverance, and unwavering dedication, Suresh's engineering colleges flourished, attracting students from far and wide. He later did his doctorate and that earned him much admiration. His commitment to excellence earned him a reputation as a visionary leader in the field of education, and his colleges became synonymous with innovation and academic excellence. But amidst all his success, Suresh never forgot his roots or the friends with whom he had developed long lasting relationship and helped along the way. Vishal remained grateful to Suresh for the role he had played in his life and often reminisced about their days aboard the floating dry dock.

As the years went by, Suresh's chain of engineering colleges in NCR Delhi continued to thrive, and he rose to even greater heights, leaving an indelible mark on the world of education and inspiring countless others to follow in his footsteps. And though his journey had taken him far including into politics from the rolling waves of the ocean, Suresh never forgot the lessons he had learned at sea - lessons of camaraderie, resilience, and the power of partnership to weather any storm.

For Vishal's other friend and batchmate from Electrical Ashok Kaushal, the Indian Navy was more than just a career—it was a calling, a way of life. And as he looked ahead to the future, he knew that whatever challenges lay in store, he would face them with courage, determination, and the unwavering commitment to serve his country with honour and integrity.

Once he completed his fifteen years initial assignment with Indian Navy, he ventured into civil life. He went on to work on many construction projects for Hospitals, Hotels & Resorts, and few other projects within India and abroad. He worked both on projects construction and operations side. His last known assignment was as Director (Engineering) - Asia Pacific for a prestigious chain of hotels.

EXAM: Sailing Through Generations

Once a year, a unique gathering takes place that echoes with the tales of engines noise and vibration, wires crackling, and ship's hulls creaking against the sea or naval sorties on board ships. This is no ordinary reunion; it is the Ex-Artificers Meet, fondly known as EXAM, where the ex-naval artificer engineers, converge to share stories, reminisce, and celebrate the bonds forged in the crucible of naval engineering.

From the bustling streets of Mumbai to the serene shores of Goa, to other prominent town like Mysore, Amritsar, Kochi, Puri, Jaipur each year saw a different city play host to this illustrious gathering. The location changes every year, a deliberate choice to explore the diverse landscapes of India and, occasionally, foreign shores. Naval artificers, ranging between age from 35 to 90-plus years old, descended upon the chosen venue, eager to reconnect with old comrades and share stories of their time in service.

It is more than just a reunion; it is a voyage through time, connecting generations of naval artificers who had once sailed together on different seas. When EXAM unfolds in the different city every year, the rhythm of the region provides a fitting backdrop to the stories of the seas shared by veterans from around the globe. The attendees range from spiritly 35-year young to seasoned veterans well into their 90s. Each face bore the weathering of time, etched with the experiences of a life dedicated to naval engineering.

As veterans' trickle into the venue, the air gets thick with nostalgia and camaraderie. Stories of distant shores, challenging repairs at sea, and the intricate dance of machinery filled the room. The laughter is always hearty, and the bonds, forged in the bowels of naval vessels, proven unbreakable even with the passage of time. The highlight of EXAM is not just the camaraderie among the retired engineers but the presence of the younger generation, the torchbearers of the naval artificer legacy. Sons and daughters accompanying their veteran fathers, eager to absorb the tales of the sea and the lessons learned through a lifetime of service. For the veterans, it is a chance to pass on their knowledge, ensuring that the flame of naval engineering burned brightly in the hearts of those who would carry the legacy forward.

The event has a kaleidoscope of activities, from technical discussions on the evolution of naval engineering to cultural evenings filled with music and dance. The EXAM become a melting pot of experiences, where the sea stories of an octogenarian resonated with the aspirations of a young who are just beginning their journey. At times fellow artificer from other countries who have trained here, keep the thread of bond intact by joining.

On first day, as the sun sets over, casting hues of orange and pink across the horizon, the EXAM participants gather for a solemn ceremony to honour those who had well passed their final voyage. The roll call of departed comrades echo through the evening breeze, a poignant reminder of the sacrifices made in the service of the seas. For three days artificers young or old alike accompanied with wives explore and tour each city, savour food, and mingle over the cocktails together strengthening existing bond.

The climax of EXAM is the grand dinner every evening. Awards are handed out, speeches are given, and tears shed for those who had sailed into the eternal seas. The collective pride in their shared heritage reverberated through the room. The cultural program and highlights of the host city are celebrated.

EXAM is more than just a reunion; it is a living testament to the enduring spirit of naval artificers. It is a celebration of the bonds formed in the crucible of naval engineering, a passing of the torch to the next generation, and a reminder that, though the seas may change, the heart of a naval artificer remained steadfast, forever anchored in the call of the sea.

On the departing day, everyone with a renewed pledge to meet again, leaves with happy memories to cherish until next year EXAM. Vishal, like all others promises to be back next year to meet his partner comrades.

PART 4

MARITIME CONSULTING & DOCUMENTARY FILMS

Sailing Through Frames: Journey into Filmmaking

In the Feb of 1997, after nearly two decades as a naval engineer, Vishal was standing at the crossroads of his career. With the sea breeze still lingering in his memory, he decided to embark on a new and unexpected venture - documentary filmmaking.

Vishal's interest in filmmaking had always been a quiet flame within him, waiting for the right moment to burst into a creative blaze. That moment arrived when he discussed it with his old school friend Naveed, trained in film direction from the prestigious Pune Film Institute. He had watched him shootings films whenever Vishal was at Delhi while in Navy and always had a desire to be part of it someday.

Naveed listened intently as Vishal spoke of his passion for storytelling and his fascination with the world of cinema. Inspired by his friend's enthusiasm, Naveed suggested that Vishal try his hand at documentary filmmaking, leveraging his unique perspective as a former naval engineer to shed light on untold stories from the world of maritime. Excited by the prospect, Vishal jumped at the opportunity and, with Naveed's guidance, embarked on a journey into the world of documentary filmmaking.

Armed with a Sony U-matic video camera and a vision, Vishal and Naveed with his team of professionals set out to document the unseen facets of naval life. Naveed was an experienced hand and had already worked for few documentaries and short films showcasing army and police organisations earlier. The duo made elaborate plans to capture ports, shipping, and naval history, creating a tapestry of narratives that painted a vivid picture of life at sea.

The first few months were a whirlwind of learning for Vishal. Naveed patiently guided him through the intricacies of cinematography, storytelling, and editing. Vishal, ever the quick learner and a thinker, embraced the challenge with the same determination that had fuelled his naval career and would do lot of research on subject varying from maritime history, wildlife, and historical places of interest.

Vishal's firsthand experiences and Naveed's artistic finesse blended seamlessly, giving the documentary a unique and authentic touch. They worked closely with Door Darshan at Delhi and did start filming short documentaries on subjects pre-approved for telecast. As the project progressed, Vishal discovered a newfound appreciation for the power of storytelling through the lens. With Naveed by his side, the editing tables became his tool to immortalize the unspoken works with, the silent victories, and the enduring spirit.

As Vishal basked in the glow of his newfound success, he knew that he had found his calling. Along with Naveed, he embarked on a new chapter in his life, using his skills as a documentary filmmaker to shine a light on the untold stories of the world around him and inspire others to pursue their passions, no matter where life may take them.

Interestingly, during one such occasion of research on the Ports of India for his documentary, Vishal incidentally met Captain JS Gill, Master Mariner, a retired Deputy Director General of Shipping and Nautical Advisor to Government with a storied career. The discussion varied from filming work in hand to Ports and finally to Vishal past career with Navy. Captain Gill found Vishal an energetic man with substantial knowledge on varied subject and proposed him to assist him in his consultancy on maritime subjects. Vishal just could not miss newfound opportunity to expand his horizon alongside film making.

Seas of Wisdom- A New Horizon

This time, the sea of possibilities extended beyond the navy, and he decided to navigate the realm of port and shipping policies. But such uncharted waters required guidance, and Vishal found a seasoned captain to help him navigate the complexities of the shipping industry. Recognizing Vishal's potential, Captain Gill extended a guiding hand, offering his wealth of knowledge and experience to help Vishal transition into the world of maritime research, drafting notes, policy formulation and advisory roles.

Their journey began with countless conversations in Captain Gill's office in basement of his house in Delhi, surrounded by nautical books, charts and maritime artifacts. Captain Gill, with his salt-and-pepper beard and a lifetime of experiences, shared tales of the sea and the intricacies of maritime policies. Vishal, eager to absorb every drop of wisdom, listened intently, his eyes lighting up with newfound understanding. In Captain Gill's office, Vishal experienced working on the computers for the first time. He started to learn and enjoy newfound tool to learn and work with enthusiasm.

Under Captain Gill's mentorship, Vishal dived deep into the nuances of port and shipping policies. Together, they navigated through the dense waters of international regulations, trade dynamics, and economic policies that shaped the maritime industry. Vishal's engineering background proved to be an asset, allowing him to grasp the technical intricacies that often-eluded policy makers.

As months passed, Captain Gill introduced Vishal to key players in the shipping industry, facilitating interactions with higher government officials, industry leaders, and members of various chambers of commerce. The seminars and meeting at FICCI, ASSOCHAM and CII gave Vishal fresh perspective, coupled with Captain Gill's seasoned insights, brought a dynamic energy to these discussions, sparking innovative ideas and pragmatic solutions. Together they often met Mr Amit Mitra, Secretary General FICCI in his office, and discussed maritime topics of interest. At times, he assisted Captain Gill with his lecture assignments at Indian Institute of Foreign Trade where he taught as a guest faculty.

Their collaborative efforts bore fruit as Vishal began to prepare important reports for different chambers of commerce to present policy changes needed. Throughout this transformation, Captain Gill stood by Vishal's side, offering encouragement and guidance. Together, they navigated the bureaucratic currents, turning challenges into opportunities and setbacks into lessons. Vishal's commitment to the cause and Captain Gill's wealth of experience proved to be a formidable combination, steering them towards success. As Vishal donned the hat of a consultant in policy formulation, he reflected on the unlikely partnership that had brought him to this point. Captain Gill, the seasoned captain, had not only shared his knowledge but also instilled in Vishal the ethos of leadership, resilience, and a deep-seated respect for the boundless possibilities that lay beyond the horizon.

And so, as Vishal continued to make impressions in the policy circles, he knew that the seas of wisdom he had sailed with Captain Gill would forever guide him on this new, uncharted journey. Together, they had transformed a premature retiree naval engineer into a beacon of influence in the maritime policies, navigating the currents of change for the betterment of the industry.

End of an Emerging Idea

By end 1997, the Indian television industry witnessed a significant shift with the entry of big and high-tech players from international broadcasters. Vishal, a small documentary filmmaker in the making, and aspiring storyteller, had been cultivating his craft in Delhi, envisioning a career in the filming with Naveed. He had cultivated connections in the local industry and was exploring avenues to expand his journey into corporate films.

However, the influx of major television networks and production houses in Mumbai, the hub of the Indian entertainment industry, presented new opportunities and challenges. The emergence of Star TV and other international players with high quality and expansive filming set ups brought a wave of innovation and high production values to the television industry. Mumbai became the epicentre of this revolution, attracting talent, resources, and creative minds from across the country. The soap opera, telefilms, and documentary work, predominantly in domain of door darshan till then started to shift to Mumbai with the advent of private TV channels. NOIDA TV studios were reduced to producing news and related programme.

Few of the regular actors, cameraman and storywriters' part of Naveed's team had decided to move to Mumbai for better prospects. Among them were some unknown names then, likes of Sakshi Tanwar, Rajeev Khandelwal, Shirish Sharma, Varun Badola, Vanya Joshi and few mores, who later made their names famous in Mumbai TV industry, after shifting there.

Recognizing the shift in the industry dynamics, Vishal faced a crucial decision: whether to stick to his plans in Delhi or venture into the thriving scene in Mumbai. But as Naveed had no plans to move, idea was shelved.

An Unforeseen Voyage: Call to Public Service

One day, while Vishal was deeply engrossed in editing his latest project, a wildlife documentary, he received interview call letter that would alter the course of his professional journey. The Union Public Service Commission (UPSC) had reached out to him for an interview for the position of a Senior Design Officer (Naval Construction) at the Coast Guard Headquarters. He had long back applied for the post but forgot since considerable time had lapsed since then.

Caught off guard by this unforeseen opportunity, Vishal hesitated for a moment. However, the intrigue of serving and contributing once again to the maritime domain rekindled his sense of duty. What made the prospect more interesting that the position was at his home city Delhi. Intrigued by the prospect of a career shift, Vishal decided to explore the opportunity further.

The UPSC examination process for the position involved a challenging interview. Determined to give it his best, Vishal immersed himself in the preparation, drawing parallels between his creative problem-solving skills in filmmaking and the technical expertise required for the role.

The day of the interview arrived, and Vishal found himself facing a panel of seasoned professionals. The panel was chaired by a senior UPSC member, Lt General (Retd.) Surinder Nath, along with technical head of

Coast Guard Service, a DIG ranking officer, and other eminent members from maritime industry.

Drawing from his diverse experiences in the Navy, balancing his naval duties with rigorous preparation for the interview, Vishal drew upon his extensive knowledge of naval construction and engineering, shipyard practices and ships repair and maintenance. As he spoke about his experiences navigating complex naval system and technologies, addressing engineering challenges at sea, and construction of naval vessels, Vishal realized the profound connection between his role as a naval engineer and the responsibilities of a Senior Design Officer. His ability to adapt to unforeseen circumstances, coupled with his knack for innovative problem-solving, resonated well with the interview panel.

His technical ability was tested to the brink with questions ranging across wide spectrum. His experience with submarine design and later at Floating Dry Dock in Navy particularly came handy for the post. The interview panel was impressed by his unique perspective on the state of shipbuilding in India, and Vishal left the room with a sense of accomplishment.

Days turned into weeks as Vishal waited anxiously for the results. To Vishal's surprise and delight, he received the news that he had been selected for the important position at Coast Guard Headquarters. The realization that he was now on the cusp of a different adventure, one that involved serving in a unique capacity, dawned upon him.

The decision to transition, from the world of documentary filming and consultancy career with Captain Gill to the disciplined realm of naval construction, was not an easy one for Vishal. Yet, as he reflected on the unexpected twist that had led him here, he embraced the change with open arms. His one and half year's journey into filmmaking and maritime consultancy marked a new chapter in his life, one that he approached with the same passion, dedication, and spirit that had defined his career in past.

PART 5

THE COAST GUARD JOURNEY

Sailing the Seas of Excellence: A Mentorship

As Vishal stepped into his new role as a Senior Design Officer (Naval Construction) at Coast Guard Headquarters, the vast expanse of responsibilities and challenges lay before him like uncharted waters. As he joined the daily morning meeting for the first time, noticed DIG Jitendra Singh, Director (Material) head of coast guard technical services, and the member who had interviewed him, was sitting across chairing the meeting. He welcomed Vishal and introduced him to the other Coast Guard officers with whom he would be working now onward.

Fate had a seasoned mentor in store for him – Commandant Arijeet Sen, Joint Director (Ship Acquisition) a highly accomplished marine engineer with a wealth of experience and a reputation for excellence. Arijeet Sen, took Vishal under his wing, recognizing the potential and enthusiasm in his new protégé. From the outset, it was clear that this mentorship would be more than just a professional relationship; it would be a transformative journey for Vishal, marked by technical expertise and administrative prowess.

In the initial days, Arijeet provided Vishal with a comprehensive overview of the Coast Guard's ship design and acquisition process. His guidance ranged from the intricacies of naval architecture to the administrative intricacies of acquiring and constructing vessels for the Coast Guard fleet. Arijeet's guiding style was anything but patient and rigorous, while ensuring that Vishal grasped the finer nuances of the maritime domain. During discussions, Commandant Sen sometimes would seek a nod from Vishal if it was same way in Navy or not. Vishal would watch and listen intensely to Sen on every technical discussion to grasp the knowledge and wisdom.

With Arijeet's guidance, Vishal dove deep into the more complexities of ship design and construction. He learned how to analyse and optimize the important aspects of a vessel construction, considering factors such as Weight Calculation, Ship Stability, Propulsion, Powering Calculation, and mission-specific requirements. Arijeet's wealth of experience became a treasure trove for Vishal, who absorbed knowledge like a sponge, eager to apply it in his new role.

Beyond the technical aspects, Arijeet also instilled in Vishal the importance of effective project management. Under his mentorship, Vishal learned to navigate the bureaucratic channels associated with acquiring new ships and boats. From machinery selection, procurement to regulatory compliance, Arijeet's administrative acumen provided a holistic understanding of the ship acquisition process. Arijeet's mentorship was not confined to the office; it extended to the field, where Vishal got firsthand experience in overseeing the construction and testing phases of Coast Guard vessels. Arijeet emphasized the significance of collaboration, encouraging Vishal to build strong relationships with shipyards, vendors, and regulatory authorities.

As Vishal flourished under Arijeet's mentorship, he began to contribute significantly to the Coast Guard's ship design and acquisition projects. His confidence grew, and his ability to navigate the intricacies of maritime engineering and administration became increasingly refined. His acumen was now appreciated at other department of Headquarters associated with ship acquisition such as Plans and Operations. The culmination of this mentorship was evident in the successful acquisition and commissioning of a state-of-the-art Hovercrafts, High Speed Interceptor Boats, Fast Patrol Vessels and Offshore Patrol Vessel for the Coast Guard. Vishal had transformed from a novice ship design officer into a capable and confident professional, ready to take on the challenges of the maritime world.

As Vishal sailed the seas of excellence, first under Arijeet Sen's guidance and later with other accomplished Coast Guard officers who replaced him, Vishal carried with him not just technical expertise but also the values of leadership, collaboration, and dedication. The mentorship had not only shaped Vishal's career but had ignited a passion for service to the nation and the maritime domain. Arijeet Sen, the beacon in Vishal's professional journey, had not only groomed a ship design officer but had fostered a legacy of maritime excellence.

Navigating Waters of Excellence: Odyssey in Ship Acquisition

Vishal's tenure as the Senior Design Officer at the Coast Guard had evolved into a seven-year odyssey marked by challenges, triumphs, and the continuous quest for excellence. From Hovercrafts to Oil Spill Response vessels, Fast Patrol Vessels, Interceptor Boats to Offshore Patrol Vessels, Vishal had been through all these ship acquisition projects with acumen, precision, and an unwavering commitment to maritime safety and security.

In the early years of his tenure, Vishal faced the intricacies of acquiring Hovercrafts for the Coast Guard, a unique and specialized fleet designed to navigate challenging coastal terrains. His technical prowess and attention to detail came to the forefront as he worked closely assisting Sen in technical evaluations of bids from many participating shipyards and took part in deliberation with hovercraft designer and engineers. Knowledge gained in the process of dealing with foreign shipyard leading to signing of Contract and Building specification gave immense sense of satisfaction and insight of ship's acquisition process to Vishal.

Interceptor Boats, a high-speed boat, became another focal point for Vishal's expertise. In the pursuit of securing coastal borders, meticulously designed vessels that were not only swift and agile but also equipped with state-of-the-art technology for desired speed, surveillance, and interception. The entire acquisition process was full of intense moments, from preventing lobbies to influence the selection process to deep technical deliberation with bidding shipyards and scrutinising technical data submitted by shipyard for meeting the RFP requirements.

He was overwhelmed to experience the knowledge and skill of Commandant Sen as he would humble the most experience of technocrat from shipyards and designers during technical discussion. Vishal's assistance and dedication in acquisition of Interceptor Boat project and later managing the project execution after the contract was awarded to shipyard, had enhanced the Coast Guard's operational capacities which earned Vishal accolades and further solidified his reputation as true professional.

The acquisition of Oil Spill Response Vessels presented a different set of challenges. This project has been on table since long in the list of planned vessels. Directorate of Plan and Directorate of Material had worked closely and after two failed attempts, steered it to release of RFP by Ministry of Defence in 2003. When the bids started to pour in from Shipyards in collaboration with foreign shipyard. It was time to evaluate technical offer first. Technical Evaluation Committee was formed under chairmanship of DIG Sushil Kumar Garg, Principal Director (Material) with members as Commandant Parmanand, Jt. Director (Ship Acquisition), a seasoned naval architect along with other technical and operational members. Vishal as senior design officer was an integral part as usual in the committee.

The committee delved into the complex process of examining each bid before calling for discussions. The scrutiny and questioning by Parmanand and team, prolonged technical discussion and calling for supporting documents for claims made in the bids, were all an exposure at different level for Vishal. He would in spare time explore the world of marine environmental protection, discussing with experts and system manufacturers to learn about required equipment to handle oil spills effectively. His strategic thinking and innovative solutions earned him recognition. He was by now master in documenting entire technical discussion and the processing it for preparation of technical report.

With time he dwelt into other acquisition projects of Fast Patrol Vessels, Offshore Patrol Vessels, and more of Interceptor Boats later. In the pursuit of securing coastal borders, he meticulously worked his way in handling vessels that were equipped with state-of-the-art technology. Vishal's dedication and commitment contributed to enhancing the Coast Guard's operational capacities and earned him accolades and further solidified his reputation.

An Inquisitive International Collaboration

The entire journey of ship acquisition at coast guard was full of technical exchanges and knowledge sharing with multiple shipyards both Indian and foreign. Indian PSUs and private shipyards came with design tie up with experienced foreign shipyards.

Deliberation for Hovercraft project was with Indian public sector shipyard who had come in collaboration with Griffin's Hovercraft from UK, ABS Hovercraft from Sweden and Almaz from Russia

For Interceptor boats, interaction included with Israel Shipyard Ltd another one other Israeli firm Israel Aircraft Industries (IAI) Ramata, Textron from USA, Thornycroft from Australia, Colombo Dockyard Ltd, BMT Nigel Gee from UK,

Fast Patrol Vessel project was deliberated with Singapore Technology Marine, and Thornycroft, Australia and Goa Shipyard Ltd among others.

Oil Spill Response Vessel, the expert shipyards included Ulstein, Norway (Later known as Roll Royce Marine, Norway) and Damen Shipyard, Netherland.

For Offshore Patrol Vessels, the notable foreign shipyard or designer who came with Indian PSUs such as Cochin Shipyard Ltd, Garden Reach Shipbuilders and ABC Shipyard were Iv Nevesbu from Netherlands, Damen shipyard, Netherland, Fincantieri from Italy, Aker Kvaerner Marine from Canada

Throughout the acquisition process, Vishal's acumen evolved not just in the technical intricacies of ship design but also in the art of project management once contract was signed with the shipyards. Projects were overall managed by coast guard technical officers posted at headquarter for execution. Vishal was responsible to manage the Interceptor Boats project in addition to few other for execution. The success of these strategic ship acquisition projects not only fortified the Coast Guard's capabilities but also boosted Vishal's confidence and stature within the organisation.

Navigating the Seas of Innovation: Ship Equipment

As Vishal had settled into his role at the Coast Guard Headquarters, he found himself at the forefront of many activities. With the Coast Guard's ambitious plans for fleet expansion and modernization underway, ship equipment suppliers from around the globe lined up at Directorate, eager to showcase their products for consideration in the new acquisition plan.

Vishal's desk became a hub of activity, representatives from various companies vying for attention. Each day brought a new wave of presentations, catalogues, and pitches, as suppliers sought to impress their products innovations and technological advancements. Vishal would arrange regular presentation from these suppliers for the benefit of coast guard community and senior officers for updates.

From state-of-the-art Marine Engines, Propulsion System, Diesel Generators, Integrated Machinery Control System, Marine Switch Boards, Navigation & Communication Systems, STPs, RO Plants, Deck Machineries, Air Condition & Refrigeration to many other cutting-edge systems and technology, Vishal was inundated with a dizzying array of products and solutions. With his keen eye for detail and his deep understanding of naval engineering principles, he meticulously evaluated each offering weighing its potential.

But amidst the flurry of activity, Vishal remained focused and composed, navigating through the sea of information with clarity and precision. He took the time to listen to supplier's pitch, asking probing questions and seeking to understand the unique value proposition of their products. Drawing on his years of experience, Vishal carefully learned about the product against Coast Guard's specific requirements, analysing and comparing life cycle cost and hence ensuring that only the most suitable solutions were suggested for further evaluation.

Despite the pressure and intensity of the process, Vishal remained steadfast in his commitment to excellence. With his in-depth study and recommendations, Vishal presented his findings to the Coast Guard's leadership headed by Principal Director (Material), outlining the strengths and capabilities of supplier and making a compelling case for their inclusion in the new acquisition plan.

Seas of Success: Role in Coast Guard Ship Construction

Vishal was at the helm of new ship acquisition and construction projects that would shape the future of the Coast Guard's fleet. Managing such multifaceted endeavours required not only technical prowess but also an adept ability to coordinate and interact with various stakeholders. The challenge included identification of capable shipyards for each specific project that will meet the Coast Guard's stringent specifications. Aim was to establish partnerships with shipyards that shared the Coast Guard's commitment to excellence.

Vishal as project officer maintained constant line of communication with the onsite Coast Guard Overseeing Team about every aspect of the construction process and progress. Regular meetings, clear communication channels, and an atmosphere of collaboration were the cornerstones of their success. Every design drawing and equipment proposed by shipyard were scrutinised at coast guard headquarters and approved at Directorate of Material.

The importance of engaging with classification societies was not lost in the mind of Vishal, to ensure that the vessels met the stringent safety and performance standards. Consultations with classification societies and referring to Class rule book became a routine part of the project timeline.

The interaction with equipment manufacturers was equally crucial. Vishal, armed with extensive available database and knowledge, had to ensure that machinery and systems proposed by shipyard comply the building Specification before they are technically cleared for installation. From Engines, Propulsion, Generators, Davits, Cranes, Communication, and Navigation systems to safety equipment, each was technically examined and deliberated in detail with manufacturers, to guarantee that each piece of equipment met the Coast Guard's specifications.

The construction phase brought Vishal to the shipyards, where he forged strong relationships with the personnel responsible for bringing the designs to life. His hands-on approach, combined with his technical expertise, endeared him to the shipyard teams. Vishal's ability to communicate effectively and resolve issues in real-time fostered a collaborative spirit, ensuring that the construction process remained on schedule.

As the projects neared completion, meticulous attention to detailed check became even more critical during approval of trial protocols. Overseeing team recommended draft protocol as prepared by shipyard that laid down criteria for the inspections, harbour and sea trials and performance tests to guarantee that each vessel met the Coast Guard's operational requirements.

The successful completion of each ship construction project not only bolstered the Coast Guard's capabilities but also solidified Vishal's reputation as a seasoned Project Officer. His ability to navigate the intricate web of shipyards, overseeing teams, classification societies, and equipment manufacturers demonstrated his technical ability and project management skills.

Ship's Hull Protection- Paint Technology

In the year 2003, at the Coast Guard headquarters, Vishal, found himself engaged in an unprecedented task. Alongside him was Commandant

Parmanand, a Naval Architect, whose expertise would leave an indelible mark on the Coast Guard's technical landscape.

The challenge at hand was to draft the first-ever paint policy for all Coast Guard ships. It was a meticulous endeavour that required the amalgamation of technical mastery, practical knowledge, and an acute understanding of the marine environment. Vishal and Commandant Parmanand were entrusted with the responsibility of formulating a comprehensive and effective paint scheme that would not only protect the coast guard vessels but also ensure a uniform and aesthetically pleasing appearance.

The duo decided to embark on a thorough exploration of the best international marine paint manufacturers, aiming to select a combination that would stand the test of time in the harsh maritime conditions. After careful consideration, they narrowed down their options to only three renowned companies among existing suppliers to Coast Guard - Jotun Paints, Sigma Paints, and International Paints with sufficient presence in Indian Market. They ensured that identified paint have the valid type of approval certificate from Ship Classification Societies

The process of selecting the ideal paint scheme was an intricate web of technical discussions, research, and studying testing results. The duo engaged in lengthy deliberations, pouring over the nuances of each paint manufacturer's products, considering factors such as lasting durability, anti-corrosion properties, compliances to marine environmental regulation in force, costs, and application process. As the discussions and trials unfolded, a consensus emerged, and a comprehensive paint policy began to take shape. The paint scheme incorporated inter compatible products of equivalence properties from Jotun Paints, Sigma Paints, and International Paints, each playing a specific role in ensuring the longevity and protection of Coast Guard vessels. The meticulous efforts culminated in the finalization of the Coast Guard's first ever comprehensive paint policy in 2003. The policy outlined the specific use of paints from the chosen international manufacturers for each class of ship and boats, detailing the type of paint, its properties, and application process.

Technical acumen of both Commandant Parmanand and Vishal proved to be an invaluable combination. The Coast Guard's vessels not only stood resilient against the elements but also boasted a uniform and professional appearance.

Commandant Parmanand's trajectory continued to soar, later ascending to the position of the Deputy Director General (Material & Maintenance) at Coast Guard Headquarters. Meanwhile, Vishal's legacy as a Senior Design Officer remained etched in the enduring protection and aesthetic appeal of the Coast Guard's fleet, a testament to the impact that thoughtful and collaborative decision-making could have on maritime operations.

State of Art High Speed Boats -A Challenge

Vishal found himself at the epicentre of a pivotal project. Tasked with acquisition of ten new high-speed Interceptor Boats, his expertise and meticulous approach would soon be tested for the transformative moment in the Coast Guard's procurement processes. These boats were the upgraded version of two similar boat acquired by Coast Guard earlier.

From financial year 2002-03 onward, all defence acquisition came under newly formed Defence Procurement Board at the Ministry of Defence. Joint Secretary (Acquisition Manager) and Technical Manager (Maritime) looked after acquisition wing for maritime division. It faced its first complete acquisition case with coast guard's Interceptor Boats project for the process of inviting tender. The draft RFP document for the project became the centrepiece of scrutiny and consultation during the procurement board's sessions. The meticulous detailing and thorough internal consultations showcased the Coast Guard's commitment to precision and transparency in its procurement processes.

The responsibility bestowed upon Vishal was no ordinary one – he was appointed as the project officer for this critical acquisition. His first task was to draft a model comprehensive guidelines specifications as technical part of qualitative requirements (QR) that would be embedded in the Request for Proposal (RFP) document for inviting bids from shipyards. The commercial part of RFP was mainly the responsibility of Plans Directorate and Vishal coordinated with his counterpart in the Plans to jointly steer the project.

Requirement varying from role and mission, maritime operations to naval architectural, engineering, electrical, communications, logistics and other aspects reflecting diverse needs of the Coast Guard's mission were included in the draft technical specifications. Through detailed scrutiny and collaborative discussions among various directorates within coast guard headquarters, and after consensus, the specifications were frozen. The guiding specifications meticulously outlined the operational capabilities, equipment, and design parameters required for the high-speed Interceptor Boats. This document would not only guide shipyards in their bids but bring all participating shipyard technically at par. This RFP if approved, would also serve as a model for all future acquisitions within the Coast Guard once approved.

As the guiding specifications took shape, they represented a significant leap forward in the Coast Guard's approach to procurement. It was not just about acquiring vessels; it was about tailoring each acquisition to meet the specific demands of Coast Guard operations. The Defence Procurement Board, recognizing the robustness of the RFP along with guideline technical specifications, approved the acquisition.

Later, the bids evaluation by the technical committee under the chairmanship of Principal Director (Material) and other members including Vishal, was completed and recommended for price bid opening based on qualification matrix. CG teams efforts for Interceptor Boats project had not only contributed to the successful acquisition of ten high-speed Interceptor Boats but had also set a new standard for future acquisitions through TM (Maritime) being its first case.

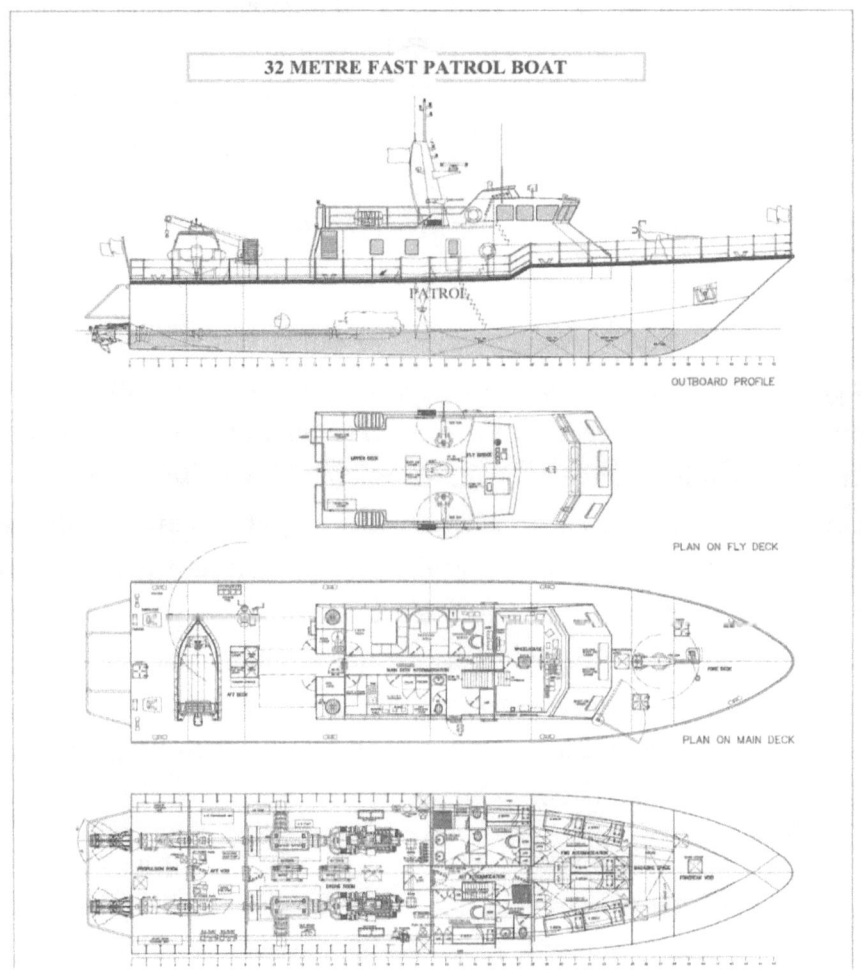

A typical High-Speed Boat

Offshore Patrol Vessel - Acquisition of Excellence

In the Coast Guard headquarters, at the heart of an ambitious new acquisition project of six Offshore Patrol Vessels (OPVs), Vishal once again found himself closely working under DIG Sushil Garg, Principal Director (Material) and Commandant Shekhar, Joint Director (Ship Acquisition) and was entrusted with a task that would test the depths of his capabilities. The project was no ordinary feat – it involved drafting detailed guiding specifications as part of RFP for the new OPVs. This was more complicated and demanding in nature compared to his earlier project of Interceptor Boats. DIG Garg, recognizing Vishal's potential and unwavering commitment, placed his faith in him, providing an opportunity to showcase his ability and leadership.

As Vishal delved into the project, he embraced the challenge with vigour and determination. Drawing upon his years of experience and the mentorship of DIG Sen, Vishal worked on a project that not only met the rigorous standards of the Coast Guard but also incorporated innovative features to enhance operational efficiency and adaptability. Throughout the process, Vishal regularly sought guidance and direction from Director (Material) and Joint Director (Ship Acquisition), whose sage advice and wealth of knowledge became invaluable assets in refining the concept design. The engagement with intense discussions, exploring various possibilities, and aligning the vessel's specifications with the Coast Guard's mission objectives.

As the project advanced, Vishal dived into the intricate task of Guideline Specifications for the Offshore Patrol Vessel. He left no stone unturned, meticulously outlining the technical specifications, performance criteria, and quality standards that would guide the shipbuilding process. Vishal's attention to detail and commitment to excellence mirrored the high standards acquired throughout his career at Coast Guard. When nearing completion, Vishal presented his work with a mix of pride and anticipation. Once the draft RFP with guiding technical specifications were ready and compiled, the project was processed further by Principal Director (Plan) for the Ministerial approval.

As time passed by, Vishal's area of responsibility grew, he continued to display his potential which even later brought laurel and appreciation when coast guard bestowed him with Director General's Commendation.

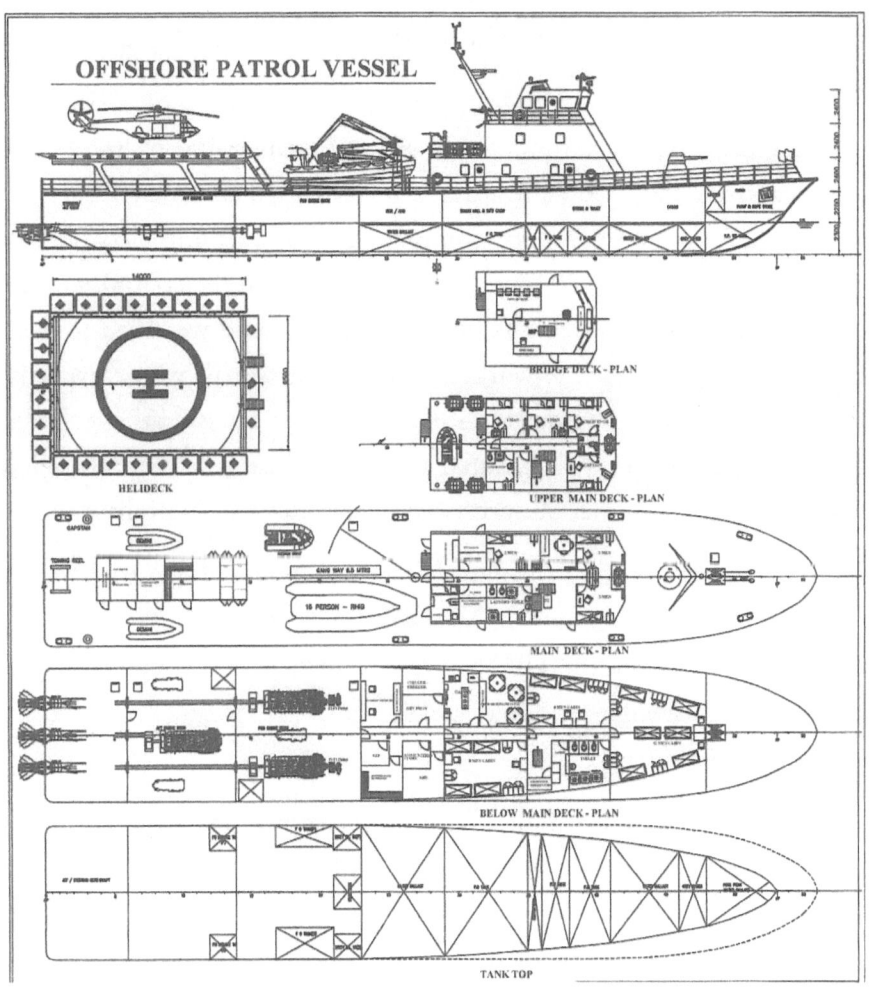

A Typical Plan of an Offshore Patrol Vessel

Evaluating Right Shipyard -Project OPV

The Offshore Patrol Vessel Project was cleared by acquisition wing and tender floated to qualified Indian shipyards. Vishal as usual found place in the technical committee as member. After long time, Vishal was to closely work under the watchful eye of his mentor, DIG Arijeet Sen, who was now serving as Principal Director (Fleet Maintenance) and nominated as Technical Committee Chairman for the OPV acquisition project. Vishal was entrusted with a task that would test the depths of his capabilities.

He took on the critical responsibility of analysing technical bids received from multiple shipyards. On recommendation of DIG Sen, another naval architect Deputy Commandant Raju, serving at coast guard overseeing organisation in Mumbai, was included in the committee, and called on deputation. This was his first such role and was keen to learn the intricacy involved. He worked closely with Vishal, whose expertise over the year working under DIG Arijeet Sen's in assessing the technical nuances of ship proposals ensured that the Coast Guard would select vessels that not only met but exceeded operational expectations.

The seasoned marine engineer Sen was hugely impressed by the thoroughness and precision of Vishal's efforts, when he went through RFP for the OPV project. DIG Sen recognized Vishal's potential not just as a skilled naval engineer but as a leader capable of taking on significant responsibilities.

As bids started to pour in, technical committee started inviting shipyards for discussions. Some of the shipyard offered their proposal in collaboration with reputed foreign shipyard. Technical committee analysed ship's weight calculations, hull resistance to motion, speed to powering requirement, and propellers design data. Team scrutinized entire technical specifications to ensure that the shipyards chosen had the efficient ship design to offer that were not only well-suited for the vessel's intended purpose but also optimized for efficiency.

As all shipyards had offered completely new design without a proven ship in past, one fundamental question for team was to check the ship's powering carefully- whether the effective power to drive the ship is delivered at the propulsive unit. Technical team paid particular attention to set of parameters that determined the propulsion performance. They scrutinized the details related to the design of propellers, its quasi-propulsive coefficient (QPC), also examining other factors such as blade pitch, diameter, and material. The meticulous evaluation of these criteria was crucial in determining the propeller's effectiveness in providing optimal thrust while minimizing energy consumption.

Transmission losses in the shafting system became another focal point for analysis. Recognizing that power transmission efficiency was paramount for the vessel's overall performance, and meticulously verified whether the shipyards had considered all modes of operational profile. From standard cruising to more demanding operational modes, team ensured that the proposed shafting systems were designed to minimize energy losses and maximize power utilization. Understanding the complexities of power reductions along the shafting system, team ensured that the proposed systems were not only robust but also capable of maximizing power efficiency.

Vishal's expertise allowed him to go beyond surface-level assessments. They engaged in in-depth discussions with the bidding shipyards, seeking clarification on every critical system, machineries and the design considerations for the propulsion system. They verified and ensured that sufficient design margins are available for the future upgradation. Shipyard were asked to submit past model test report of a similar design vessel if any to analyse. His detailed queries on technical offer, vetted by DIG Sen, aimed to unearth the shipyards' commitment to delivering vessels that not only adhered to the Coast Guard's specifications but also demonstrated an understanding of the complex interplay between propulsion efficiency and power transmission.

Propulsion engines specifications, suitable application (whether for high speed or medium speed operation), or if complying to ship's operational profile, maximum continuous engine power delivered, torque, fuel consumption rate and most importantly the life cycle costing were analysed deeply. Committee ensured that the engines were appropriately sized and powered for the intended application and has the valid type of approval certificate from any international classification society from marine application.

In addition to propulsion, team paid special attention to the electrical power to see if diesel generators collective power is aligned with ship's total power requirement and has adequate reserve power. They examined whether the proposed generator capacity adequately covered the ship's power load in various modes – from standard cruising to heightened surveillance, or external firefighting mode or harbour load or emergency situations. This careful consideration aimed to guarantee that the vessel would have reliable power, essential for its diverse operational needs.

As the technical bids were evaluated, Vishal collaborated closely at each stage with fellow committee members, leveraging their collective expertise to arrive at a comprehensive recommendation. The effectiveness of each proposal was carefully weighed against the Coast Guard's operational requirements, and only those shipyards that demonstrated a thorough understanding of requirement specified in guiding specifications emerged as strong contenders. As a standard, all essential and desirable criteria were verified if it met the RFP and matrix drawn among shipyard to identify the qualifying shipyard. The technical committee reviewed the draft report in detail and arrived at consensus before finalising it.

Ultimately, Vishal's role as a senior design officer and as technical committee member went beyond the technical details; it encompassed a commitment to selecting vessels that would serve the Coast Guard with unparalleled efficiency. With DIG Sen's commendation ringing in his ears, Vishal looked towards the future with newfound confidence. The success of the OPVs acquisition project marked a milestone in his career, solidifying his reputation as an officer capable of steering ambitious endeavours. As he continued to grow and contribute to the Coast Guard's mission, Vishal remained grateful for the guidance and trust bestowed upon him by DIG Sen.

Key Result Area - Vishal's Legacy

In Coast Guard Vishal, had by now become synonymous with technical excellence and reliability. His reputation as a meticulous and thorough evaluator had been earned over the years through his role in the TEC, where he scrutinized technical bids from participating shipyards for various projects.

Vishal's attention to detail, analytical prowess, and in-depth knowledge of naval construction made him a trusted and invaluable asset to the technical team. His commitment to upholding the highest standards in technical evaluation had earned the confidence of his superiors, directors, and colleagues alike. Vishal's role was not just about ticking boxes; it was about ensuring that every technical aspect of a bid aligned seamlessly with the Coast Guard's stringent requirements.

The ability to identify potential issues and recommend solutions showcased Vishal's dedication to the success of each project. He never hesitated to approach his superior for slightest of doubt and took their advice seriously. Whether it was evaluating ship designs, scrutinizing machinery specifications, or ensuring that all systems were in perfect harmony, Vishal approached each task with a sense of responsibility and professionalism that left a lasting impression. His thoroughness and expertise had become a hallmark of the Technical Evaluation Committees. As projects came and went, Vishal's seniors in the organization consistently expressed their satisfaction and appreciation for the results he delivered. His role had evolved into a key position within the Coast Guard's technical team, and his reputation for excellence extended beyond the evaluation committees.

In the fast-paced and complex world of naval construction, Vishal's work became a cornerstone for right decisions reinforcing his position as a key figure in the organization. The confidence placed in him by his superiors reflected not just his technical acumen but also his unwavering commitment to ensuring that every vessel acquired by the Coast Guard met the highest standards of safety, efficiency, and operational capability.

Blessing in Disguise- A God Send Opportunity

Shri Ram Kamra, an aged and highly accomplished Naval Architect and Director (Technical) at ABC Shipyard, had spent decades navigating the intricate waters of shipbuilding and naval architecture. His keen insights and vast experience had not only shaped their shipyard into a reputable name in the industry but had also cultivated lasting relationships with professionals across the maritime domain.

Among those professionals was Vishal, a Ship Constructor and Naval Architect with an impressive track record at the Coast Guard. Shri Kamra had often found himself engaged in technical deliberations with Vishal during the bidding processes for Coast Guard ships. Over the years, Shri Kamra had come to appreciate Vishal's expertise, dedication, and unwavering commitment to excellence.

The Managing Director of ABC Shipyard and Shri Kamra both had a vision for expanding the shipyards into major defence shipbuilding unit. Recognizing this, Kamra saw an opportunity to elevate the shipyard's standing by building more defence vessels in the industry and thought of roping in suitable professional likes of Vishal on board.

One day, while Vishal was on official visit to ABC shipyard, Shri Kamra extended an invitation to Vishal for a cup of tea in his office after the meeting. Curiosity mingled with anticipation as Vishal stepped into Kamra's office, where they exchanged greetings and engaged in a candid conversation over tea about their shared experiences in the maritime sector. During the discussion, Shri Kamra expressed his admiration for Vishal's work at the Coast Guard and his contributions during the bidding processes. He acknowledged Vishal's deep understanding of ship construction, and the intricate requirements of defence shipbuilding.

"In you, Vishal, I see not just a naval architect and ship constructor but a professional with the vision and expertise to lead our defence shipbuilding endeavours," Shri Kamra stated.

Vishal listened intently, feeling a surge of validation for his years of hard work and dedication. Shri Kamra continued, outlining his vision for the shipyard's expansion into defence shipbuilding and the pivotal role he envisioned for Vishal in making that vision a reality.

"I would like to offer you a key position in our shipyard, overseeing the defence shipbuilding division as Dy. General Manager for defence projects. Your skills, experience, and innovative approach are exactly what we need to take this shipyard to new heights in the defence sector," Kamra declared.

Vishal, humbled by the offer, felt a sense of excitement and purpose. The prospect of spearheading defence shipbuilding at ABC Shipyard presented a thrilling challenge, and he decided to give it a serious thought and thanked Shri Kamra for the generous offer and for appreciating his potential. He left with a promise to revert as soon as possible.

Final Call- A Change of Track

At the Coast Guard, Vishal, after seven years of service, found himself at a crossroads. Despite his unwavering commitment and contributions to the ship construction projects, he began to sense a stagnation in his career progression. As a civilian officer in a predominantly uniformed Coast Guard environment, Vishal couldn't ignore the subtle biases that seemed to affect his chances of advancement. His file for promotion to next level of Principal Design Officer was not finding favour in the organisation.

With another sixteen years of service ahead of him for retirement age, Vishal pondered his options. The prospect of remaining in a position with no growth was disheartening, and the desire for new challenges and opportunities tugged at him. Frustration began to mount as he realized the potential within him was not being fully recognized or utilized.

Armed with Shri Kamra's proposed offer and family's consent, one summer afternoon in 2005, after careful contemplation and fuelled by the courage to pursue change, Vishal made a life-altering decision. He decided to spread his wings beyond the confines of the Coast Guard and venture into the dynamic world of the private sector. His destination? The largest private shipbuilder, ABC Shipyard, known for its ambitious projects and commitment to innovation.

As a parting interaction and thanksgiving to his mentor DIG Arijeet Sen, Vishal went to seek his blessings, who was heading as Principal Director (Fleet Maintenance) at Coast Guard Headquarter then. Once he informed him of his departure, the word expressed by him remained etched in Vishal memory "it's Coast Guard service's loss". Vishal could not have expected more from his mentor as he left with immense satisfaction of having fulfilled Sen's measure.

PART 6

ABC SHIPYARD JOURNEY

Odyssey of Corporate Voyage

As Vishal stepped into his new role in the corporate world at Mumbai office, the change was palpable. Surrounded by professionals, who embraced him with open arm and valued his experience and background, he felt a renewed sense of purpose. The shipyard, which was based in a coastal town 280 km away from Mumbai, with its vast facilities and cutting-edge technology, offered a canvas for Vishal to unleash his creativity and skills. Here he was now working alongside engineers mostly from merchant shipping and shipyard professional in charge of commercial shipbuilding projects and quickly made his place among them winning their confidence.

In his new environment, Vishal quickly adapted to the fast-paced nature of private shipyard operations. The challenges were invigorating, and Vishal's talents were finally getting the recognition they deserved. The transition also brought unexpected benefits. Vishal engaged with diverse teams, fostering collaboration and innovation. His counterpart at shipyard and in charges of ship production for his assigned projects Mr Doshi, Shankaran, Patra, all prominent professional in their field of expertise, welcomed Vishal, knowing that coming from Coast Guard, Vishal would bring along necessary skill for handling of Coast Guard's and Navy's projects. His expertise in naval construction seamlessly integrated with the shipyard's goals, and his achievements became notable milestones in the company's success.

As the years unfolded, Vishal's decision to leave the Coast Guard proved to be a catalyst for his personal and professional growth. His reputation as a skilled naval engineer and design expert reached new heights. Vishal's story became an inspiration for others who dared to step out of their comfort zones and explore uncharted territories.

Reflecting on his journey, Vishal acknowledged that leaving the Coast Guard was a difficult but necessary decision. The stagnant waters of his previous position had given way to a dynamic and thriving career in the private sector. With each passing year at ABC Shipyard, Vishal felt a profound sense of fulfilment, grateful for the courage to navigate through uncharted waters and discover the boundless possibilities that awaited him in the corporate world.

In the Heartland of Shipyard

Vishal frequented shipyard premises from Mumbai office to take stock of the projects where salty breeze carried tales of the sea in the atmosphere. Vishal found working in shipyard premises, an exciting chapter of his career. Armed with extensive exposure in managing ship construction and acquisition projects of Coast Guard and Navy, Vishal was chartering another territory, a private shipbuilding yard.

The shipyard, was a thriving hub of activity, filled with the loud sound of metals and machinery. Vishal's noticed wave of change from silent corridor of design offices and bureaucratic set up to noise of ship's fabrications, CNC plasma cutting machines, plate rolling machine, moving cranes, forklifts, heavy engineering workshops, Arc welding machines, paint shops, dry dock, and synchro lifts, shifting of ship's block and ground movement of ships from building berths to synchro lifts for launching and so on. As he took charge of managing his projects of ships from the ground up, the realisation of complexity grew.

His years in the navy had honed Vishal's skills to perfection. He understood the intricacies of naval engineering like the back of his hand. His experience with the Coast Guard had exposed him to the challenges of managing complex projects, from planning to execution. With this wealth of knowledge, Vishal was ready to navigate the uncharted waters of the private shipbuilding industry.

The first project that landed on Vishal's desk was nothing short of ambitious – the construction of three state-of-the-art Oil Spill Response Vessels of Coast Guard. The ship was to be equipped with cutting-edge technology for oil spill response, machinery automation, unmanned machinery notation and dynamic positioning system. It was dream cum true, full of pride realising that this is the same ship he was involved since concept design to tendering and technical evaluations, while working in Coast Guard and now lies the opportunity to finally build it. It was a challenging endeavour, but Vishal thrived on challenges. His point of contact at Coast Guard was his ex-colleague, an energetic Commandant Subodh Mitra, who was the project officer for OSRV and together they both worked towards fructifying it.

Vishal, as Dy General Manager (Project) armed with delegated responsibility from the senior management, embarked on to manage the project with a defined budget. With a meticulous eye for detail and a knack for inspiring his team, Vishal set out to bring his vision to life. At ABC shipyard, until now the project was looked after jointly by Rajesh Garg, an experienced Chief Engineer from shipping background and Karan Maity, a seasoned Naval Architect who had worked for long in Mazagaon dock in the past. Vishal had dealt extensively with Karan in past at coast guard, along with Director Mr Kamra, and knew him well. He relied extensively on them for carrying forward the project for shipyard. He along with Shankaran and Patra manages to re organise whole team like a well-coordinated fleet, each member a specific role based on their expertise.

The shipyard buzzed with activity as welders, engineers, and technicians worked in harmony under Patra and Vishal's overall project coordination. Design team of shipyard for hull, piping and electrical, each was headed by a selected lot of ex design engineer from public sector shipyards with vast experience in defence shipbuilding. Managing the overall design coordination between ABC Shipyard's in house design team and the ship's basic designer Rolls Royce was primarily lay with Vishal. His single point of contact for coordinating design activity with Rolls Royce Marine was Mr Knut from Norway.

Vishal had immense faith in Patra's competency and relied heavily on his handling in managing nitty gritty of project. Patra a mechanical engineer an expert with vast experience on marine engines like Wartsila and Caterpillar, and machinery installation, commissioning was constant companion and kept Vishal updated of critical issues about material or equipment which could affect the project timeline for production. They would jointly discuss with Coast Guard Overseeing Team and apprise about the progress, critical issues and to push for any pending approvals from Coast Guard.

As the construction progressed, Vishal faced unforeseen challenges that tested his leadership skills. Delays in the delivery of specialized equipment and unexpected design modifications threatened to derail the project. However, Vishal's calm demeanour and strategic problem-solving abilities in dealing with Coast Guard steered the project somewhat on course. Vishal's journey at ABC shipyard continued, and he went on to manage another challenging project of Coast Guard. This time series of high-tech Aluminium High-Speed Interceptor Boats which were his subject while working at Coast Guard and now once again lay on his lap to be built.

Subsequently, his work at shipyard followed with a naval project, and other commercial vessels projects. His reputation as a seasoned professional spread wide, attracting attention and respect from within the industry. His career graph rose rapidly at shipyard while successfully delivering on task assigned.

Fury of Monsoon Rain

The relentless rain lashed Mumbai on the night of July 26, 2005. Vishal, who had recently joined the shipyard, found himself in an unexpected and challenging situation. The city was grappling with one of the worst floods in its history, and the ABC Shipyard's Mumbai office had become a temporary refuge for those stranded.

Vishal, along with Mr. Kamra, the Director of ABC Shipyard, and two colleagues, Rajesh Garg, and Karan Maity, realized the gravity of the situation as the water levels rose rapidly outside. With roads submerged and public transportation paralyzed, leaving the office became an impossible task. There were about thirty staff members who had decided to remain in the office. As the night unfolded, the team decided to make the best of the situation. They gathered essential supplies, rationed food, and settled in for an unplanned overnight stay at the office. Despite the challenges, a sense of solidarity prevailed among the stranded colleagues. The next morning brought no relief. The city was inundated, and news reports painted a grim picture of the widespread flooding. It became evident that leaving the office would be risky, and the team decided to stay put until conditions improved.

Mr. Kamra, taking charge as the senior-most official present, planned for the team to check into a nearby hotel who wished to stay back. His decision to move to safer ground was a practical one, ensuring the team's safety and well-being. However, the challenge extended beyond the immediate group; many other staff members who had ventured out earlier were now stranded across different parts of the city. The hotel became a temporary shelter for Mr. Kamra, Vishal, Rajesh, and Karan. As the team waited for the floodwaters to recede, they monitored the situation closely, sharing updates and ensuring everyone's safety. Communication with the stranded staff became a critical aspect, and the team coordinated efforts to provide support and reassurance.

Two days later, as the city gradually began to recover, Vishal and his colleagues returned to their homes. The experience of the Mumbai flood had left an indelible mark, highlighting the importance of preparedness, resilience, and the strength of teamwork in the face of adversity. The bond forged during those challenging days remained a testament to the team spirit, with Vishal and his colleagues emerging stronger from an unexpected and unforgettable experience.

Interceptor Boats-Another Project in Lap

In the March of 2006, while Vishal was deeply engrossed with Oil Spill Response Vessel project, a fax was received at ABC Shipyard for signing of the contract for ten high speed Aluminium Interceptor Boats at Ministry of Defence. The project which had become a model RFP for the Technical Manager (Maritime) under Defence Procurement Board during 2004 and Vishal who handled it at Coast Guard as its Project Officer, was now formally assigned to ABC Shipyard.

On signing of contract, shipyard's management decided to allocate the new Coast Guard project to Vishal. Yet another project, which was virtually his since conception, now for him to build for Coast Guard like the OSRVs. For Vishal, the feeling was mixed as he pondered over the enormous faith and responsibilities laid on his shoulders by the management but was not among the type who would let go it.

The Flood Fury- A Force Majeure

The bustling shipyard had weathered many storms, both literal and metaphorical, over the years. However, nothing could have prepared them for the unprecedented challenge that lay ahead. It was a dark and stormy night in Jun 2006 when the sky opened, unleashing a torrential downpour upon the city. The rain relentlessly pounded the streets, rivers swelled, and water levels rose at an alarming rate. The city found itself submerged, and ABC Shipyard, situated near the riverbanks, bore the brunt of nature's fury. The gates of the overflowing dam were opened to save it from potential collapse and the fury was fast and enormous.

In a matter of hours, city and the shipyard were inundated under water, with water levels reaching a staggering eight feet. The once-bustling facility now resembled a vast, murky lake, and the magnitude of the disaster became apparent as the floodwaters continued to rise for two consecutive days. Machinery, equipment, and partially constructed ships were all submerged, leaving a trail of devastation in their wake. The main stores with machinery and equipment were all submerged causing damage to stored inventory. The sight of seeing the condition of ship's main engines, propeller and shafts, DG sets, pumps, and motors, all coated in thick layer of mud around was disheartening for any engineer.

The management of ABC Shipyard faced an arduous task as they surveyed the aftermath. Determined to revive the shipyard and restore operations, they mobilized a crisis management team. Mr Shankaran, Head Yard Operations and Mr Goel, Head Finance both swiftly sprang into action. The priority was the safety of the workforce, and all hands were on deck to ensure everyone was accounted for and evacuated to a secure location. Approximately thirty ships were on building berths and dock at the time of flood. Shipyard production teams and project heads from Mumbai office camped and worked nonstop days and night to ascertain the total damage. A workable plan had to be drawn out to restart the production work as soon as possible. Oil Spill Response Vessel of Coast Guard was among the projects affected by this fury and Vishal knew the consequences of not bringing the project back on track in time.

Once the immediate safety concerns were addressed, the management turned their attention to the monumental task of salvaging the shipyard. They reached out to Original Equipment Manufacturers (OEMs) to assess the damage to machinery and equipment. The OEMs, understanding the urgency of the situation, swiftly dispatched teams of experts to evaluate the condition of the submerged machinery.

The shipyard resembled a hive of activity as teams of engineers and technicians worked tirelessly to drain the water, dismantle, inspect, and recondition the affected machinery. The process was slow and meticulous, with every piece of equipment requiring thorough evaluation to ensure it met the stringent safety and quality standards required for shipbuilding. Communication was key during this challenging period. The management kept the workforce informed about the progress being made, instilling a sense of unity and purpose among the shipyard employees. Regular updates on the reconditioning and recertification process from the OEMs were shared, fostering a spirit of hope and determination.

Days turned into weeks, and gradually, in few months' times, shipyard began to emerge from the shadows of the flood. The workshops in shipyard became hub of machinery repair and reconditioning by OEMs. The reconditioned machinery and equipment received the stamp of approval from the OEMs and Classification Societies, and the shipyard's operations resumed, albeit at a slower pace initially.

Once reported to Insurance companies, the insurance surveyors were on their feet, assessing and recording every aspect of potential damage for which they will require to settle the claims. The project team for each ship was assisting them with the documentation and physical verification for proper valuation.

As the shipyard regained its footing, it became a symbol of resilience in the face of adversity. The management implemented new measures to prevent a similar catastrophe in the future, such as elevating stores of critical machinery and fortifying the shipyard against potential floods. The workforce, once demoralized, rallied together, and a renewed sense of pride permeated the shipyard.

In the end, the flood that threatened to engulf ABC Shipyard became a chapter in its history—a chapter marked not only by challenges but by the unwavering determination to overcome them. The shipyard, having weathered the storm, stood stronger than ever, a testament to the indomitable spirit of those who refused to let their dreams sink beneath the rising tide.

The Menace of Flood: Casualty Electrical Cables

As the floodwaters receded and the extent of the damage became apparent, the entire area, including the storehouses where 8000 km of imported electrical copper cables for the OSRV project were stored. The cables included all kind of power cables like Armoured, Fire Resistant, Fireproof of varied sizes, as well as Signal cables. Vishal wasted no time in springing into action. He along with Shankaran quickly mobilized a team of experts to assess the situation and devise a plan for salvaging the submerged copper cables. It was crucial to act swiftly to prevent further damage and ensure that the cables could be salvaged and used in the ship's construction.

With the help of the shipyard's dedicated workers and technicians, Vishal oversaw the painstaking process of retrieving the submerged cables from the flooded stores. Despite the challenging conditions and logistical hurdles, the team worked tirelessly to carefully extract the cables and transport them to a secure location for further inspection and testing. Consultation with Coast Guard and DNV resulted in compulsory retesting and certification before these can be authorised for use in OSRV.

Realizing the importance of ensuring the integrity and safety of the salvaged cables, Vishal in consultation with coast guard took the proactive step of sending cable samples from each type to the Central Power Research Institute (CPRI), Bangalore for thorough testing and evaluation. He stationed himself at the Institute to see through the process. The CPRI, renowned for its expertise in electrical testing and certification, conducted rigorous tests on the cables to assess their condition and suitability for reuse.

After days of meticulous testing and analysis, the CPRI delivered its verdict: the salvaged copper cables had passed the rigorous testing procedures with flying colours. With the cables deemed fit for reuse, Vishal breathed a sigh of relief, knowing that a significant hurdle had been overcome in the ship's construction plan and process in addition to saving monetary loss.

Armed with the CPRI's certification and test results, Vishal liaised with the classification society DNV (Det Norske Veritas) to seek re-certification for the salvaged cables. Through meticulous documentation and unwavering determination, Vishal ensured that all necessary protocols and standards were met, paving the way for the cables to be reintegrated into the ship's construction.

In the end, exemplary resilience in the face of adversity had not only salvaged the submerged copper cables but also ensured the successful continuation of the ship's construction.

Casualty of the Flood- Interceptor Boats

In construction of newly signed aluminium Interceptor boats project, Vishal was facing an unexpected challenge. The functioning of shipyard, known for its precision and controlled conditions, had been disrupted completely by unprecedented floods, throwing the carefully planned construction schedule of boats into disarray. The flooding had submerged sections of the shipyard, damaging many of the workshop machineries and equipment essential for the construction of the Interceptor boats. Bringing the climate control workshop back to function was utmost priority to begin the project work. Vishal, known for his resilience, assembled his team to address the aftermath of the flooding and chart a new course for the project under guidance of higher management.

The first task at hand was a thorough assessment of the damage caused by the floods and the condition of the shipyard infrastructure. The damage was extensive, requiring immediate action to salvage what could be saved and replace what was irreparably damaged. The existing plan for building interceptor boats was in disarray. New workshop machineries such as CNC cutting and number of new MIG welding machines were needed to be ordered.

As the shipyard underwent restoration and refurbishment, Vishal recalibrated the construction planning and scheduling with Mr Doshi, General Manager and in charge for the hull fabrication. It was a meticulous process that required balancing the urgency of the project with the need to ensure that every element of the construction met the high standards expected by the Coast Guard. New timelines were established, and adjustments were made to accommodate the unforeseen delays caused by the floods. Vishal worked closely with the shipyard's production team to streamline the construction process, ensuring that efficiency and quality were not compromised in the face of adversity.

An Australian Connection- Interceptor Boats

At ABC Shipyard, Vishal at the helm of the ambitious high-speed Aluminium Interceptor Boats which was being designed by an Australian firm M/s Thor Boats. It was not a small boat, but a massive 28 meter long, 6.5-meter-wide weighing 90 Tonnes, requiring a crew of ten, once completed will sail at a maximum speed of 45 knots (about 83 kmph) powered by 2 MTU engines delivering maximum of 7300 Horsepower. Realizing the complexity of the project, Vishal knew that effective coordination with key stakeholders would be essential for its success.

One of the first crucial partnerships Vishal forged was with Mr. Phil, the design and project head from Thor Boats along with its MD Mr David. Recognizing the importance of aligning the shipyard's capabilities with Thor Boat's design vision, Vishal engaged in extensive discussions with Mr. Phil in steering the project. The MD of firm David would often pitch in and together, they delved into the intricacies of the boat's design and material planning, ensuring that it not only met the Coast Guard's operational requirements but also aligned with the shipyard's production capabilities. The collaboration with Thor Boats extended beyond design discussions. Vishal worked closely with Mr. Phil speedy delivery of all essential design drawings, ensuring that the shipyard's production teams had clear and comprehensive blueprints to work with. This collaborative effort laid the foundation for a seamless integration of design and construction processes.

As the project moved forward, Vishal turned his attention to the procurement and material management aspects. Recognizing the need for specialized equipment and systems, Vishal's procurement team worked meticulously to source suppliers who could meet the stringent requirements outlined in Thor Boat's design. Negotiating contracts and ensuring timely deliveries became a significant part of Vishal's responsibilities.

To streamline the project further, Vishal had established an open line of communication with the Coast Guard Overseer assigned to monitor the project. Regular meetings and updates were organized to keep the Coast Guard informed about the project's progress. Vishal welcomed feedback and incorporated suggestions, ensuring that the end product aligned perfectly with the Coast Guard's expectations.

Within the shipyard, Vishal collaborated closely with production head of departments to coordinate the construction process. The modular construction approach, developed in collaboration with Mr. Phil, was implemented to enhance efficiency and reduce construction time. Vishal's hands-on approach ensured that any challenges faced by the production teams were addressed promptly.

Throughout the project, Vishal's role was not just that of a project manager; he became a bridge connecting design vision, procurement realities, and production capabilities. His ability to navigate the complexities of the project earned him the respect of his team, stakeholders, and the Coast Guard Overseer.

As the first Aluminium Interceptor Boat took shape on the shipyard floor, Vishal couldn't help but feel a sense of accomplishment. The successful coordination with Thor Boats for design completion, shipyard's production team, the efficient procurement processes, and the collaborative efforts with the Coast Guard had all come together. The entire project was a testament to Vishal's dedication, strategic thinking, and leadership.

Interceptor Boats During Construction in workshop

Interceptor Boats During Construction in workshop

Main Machinery Compartment   **Finishing work before Launch.**

Interceptor Boats During Sea Trials

Innovation in Propulsion Technology- Coast Guard Ships

A revolutionary project was underway – the construction of Aluminium Interceptor Boats featuring a cutting-edge water jet propulsion system. Vishal, the project head, knew that this endeavour would set a new standard for high-speed maritime operations.

The decision to implement water jet propulsion marked a departure from conventional propellers. Water jets offered enhanced manoeuvrability, reduced draft, and increased speed – critical features for the Interceptor Boats designed for swift and agile responses in coastal and open waters. The integration of the water jet propulsion system required a meticulous approach to hull design and machinery automation. The design house from Australia M/s Thor Boats ensured that the hulls were optimized for the unique characteristics of water jets. The result was a sleek and streamlined design that minimized drag and maximized efficiency. The design was further authenticated with the model testing for stability, manoeuvrability, and speed performance at a UK facility. The model test report gave very favourable results and approved by Coast Guard to proceed ahead with the construction.

To complement the propulsion system, ABC Shipyard opted for state-of-the-art automation systems of MTU engines from Germany, seamlessly integrating both engines and the water jet propulsor control. This not only provided precise control over the water jet thrust but also allowed for advanced monitoring and diagnostics, ensuring optimal performance and efficiency during operations.

The hull design incorporated a groundbreaking and first ever feature – the 3G vertical acceleration for impact strength. This design innovation ensured that the boats could withstand high-speed impacts with waves or obstacles, providing unparalleled durability and safety. The implementation of this unique feature required a delicate balance between material selection, structural design, and manufacturing processes due to impact on the increase in weight of the boat.

The water jet propulsion system, combined with the sophisticated machinery automation, transformed the Aluminium Interceptor Boats into state-of-the-art vessels. These boats exhibited unparalleled speed, agility, and resilience, making them an exceptional asset for coastal security, interception, and high-speed response missions.

Intricacies of Aluminium Hull Design and Construction

Sourcing of marine grade Aluminium AA 5083 and AA 6082 for plates and profiles in large quantity and within short schedule were difficult in India. Once the hull design was endorsed and approved by Lloyds Register, the Classification Society, complete aluminium material list was drawn out for its sourcing. The large quantity was imported in batches to begin the construction activity.

The aluminium hull construction presented a unique set of challenges and opportunities. Aluminium, known for its lightweight properties and corrosion resistance, required specialized welding techniques to ensure structural integrity and longevity. Vishal knew that the success of the project hinged on precision and expertise in Aluminium welding.

Another challenge was to create a dust free and humidity-controlled workshop. Shipyard implemented theses stringent measures. Specialized welding bays were set up, equipped with special ventilation arrangement, to ensure purity of the Aluminium surfaces within safe environment. The shipyard invested in cutting-edge welding machines capable of delivering the precise heat and control needed for Aluminium welding.

The construction process began with the preparation of Aluminium sheets, carefully cut, and shaped according to drawings and with the help of CNC cutting tapes. These sheets were then meticulously joined together as per welding plans using Metal Inert Gas (MIG) welding – a technique chosen for its ability to produce high-quality welds without compromising the structural integrity of the Aluminium. Vishal coordinated with the Shipyard production led by same team as OSRV project consisting of Mr Doshi, Patra and Shankaran and their team for the Interceptor Boat project as well. Mr Doshi an highly experience in hull production steered the aluminium hull construction with skilled manpower to perfection.

The qualified welders became artisans of metal, applying their expertise to create seamless joints that would withstand the harsh marine environment. The controlled environment minimized the risk of contamination, ensuring the purity of the aluminium welds. Mr Patra took good care of machinery installation while Shankaran as head of Yard operations provided overall support. As the hulls took shape, the shipyard's commitment to quality control remained unwavering. Non-destructive testing methods, such as ultrasonic and X-ray inspections, were employed to scrutinize every weld and ensure the structural integrity of the aluminium hulls. In addition to welding, the shipyard employed advanced techniques for aluminium surface treatment. The boats underwent a thorough process of cleaning, etching, and painting to enhance their resistance to corrosion and create a sleek and shining finish.

The final phase of the construction involved outfitting the boats with propulsion systems, other machineries, navigation and communication equipment, and other essential components. Vishal with Patra and his team collaborated closely with suppliers to integrate these elements seamlessly into the aluminium structure, maintaining the boats' overall integrity and performance.

Upon completion, the Aluminium Interceptor Boats went through the test and trail process as per laid out trial protocol and achieved required performance. The coast guard overseeing team headed by DIG

Shailendra Kumar had ensured that stringent procedures are adopted without compromise in quality and boat is completed in adherence to the approved design. He along with his team took active part in progressing the project with shipyard's team during entire construction phase. All interceptor boats were subsequently commissioned into service one by one, earning accolades for their outstanding performance. The success of the project not only showcased ABC Shipyard's commitment to innovation but also solidified their reputation as pioneers in the maritime industry.

Today, these Aluminium Interceptor Boats, with their water jet propulsion and 3G vertical acceleration hull design, remain unparalleled in their capabilities. The collaborative efforts of ABC Shipyard's team had not only pushed the boundaries of maritime technology but had also left an indelible mark on the future of high-speed naval operations.

The series of ten Aluminium hull boats that emerged from ABC Shipyard stood as a testament to the shipyard's technical prowess and commitment to innovation. Vishal's leadership, combined with the skilled craftsmanship of the shipyard's workforce, had successfully navigated the complexities of aluminium construction, setting a new standard for precision and excellence in the maritime industry. As the boats set sail, ABC Shipyard's reputation soared, marking a new chapter in their legacy of pushing the boundaries of ship construction technologies.

Payal's Symphony: A Melody of Sacrifice and Unconditional Love

In Mumbai, where the echoes of a million dreams blended with the cacophony of urban life, Vishal was entwined in the relentless rhythm of a demanding career. His days were a symphony of long commutes, meetings, and late-night working hours. Yet, amidst the crescendo of professional responsibilities, his wife, Payal, emerged as the silent conductor, orchestrating the harmony of their family life. Vishal's days were marked by the constant shuffle of paperwork on his desk. His demanding work life leaving little time for the simple pleasures of family life.

In the midst of Vishal's hectic schedule, Payal stepped into the role of a silent maestro, guiding their family through the symphony of life. Her days were a medley of school runs, college admissions, and shopping excursions for the daughters. She stood in queues under the scorching sun, patiently navigating the labyrinth of official procedures, ensuring that Monisha and Reena had the support they needed.

Payal's love became the unwavering melody that filled the void left by Vishal's frequent absences. She attended school meetings, donning the hat of both mother and father, and ensured that the daughters never felt the void of their father's presence. Late-night study sessions, giggles over ice cream, and the warmth of shared stories became her repertoire. As the girls grew older and ventured into the world of higher education, Payal continued to be their guiding light, accompanying them to college interviews, helping them choose the right courses, and providing a listening ear when the pressures of academia became overwhelming. She juggled her own responsibilities with grace, sacrificing her own needs to ensure that her daughters had the support they needed to succeed.

The Mumbai society where they lived, was a large family cultivated over the period and Payal spent her spare times either in the cultural activities or group meeting over tea. As Vishal crisscrossed the city for work, Payal held the fort at home. She juggled not only the responsibilities of parenthood but also managed their social network and friend outings. The laughter of friends echoed in their home, a testament to Payal's ability to create a nurturing space even amid her own sacrifices.

Her days were a montage of selflessness—long hours spent in the kitchen crafting favourite dishes, late-night calls to Vishal when he was away to shipyard, and early mornings preparing lunchboxes for daughters. While Vishal sailed through the demands of his career, Payal navigated the intricate channels of family life, often sacrificing her own needs for the sake of their daughters. In the quiet moments, when the city slept and the stars adorned the sky, Payal's heart swelled with a mix of pride and exhaustion. The sacrifices were countless, the challenges unending, yet her love remained a constant beacon in the storm of life.

As the years unfolded, Payal's symphony of sacrifice became the melody that defined their family. Her unwavering support allowed Vishal to pursue his dreams, knowing that the home front was secure. The sacrifices she made, the quiet battles she fought, were not lost on Vishal, who came to realize that the true heartbeat of their family was Payal's selfless love.

In the tapestry of their shared journey, Payal's sacrifices became the thread that wove together the fabric of their family. Their daughters, Monisha and Reena, grew up in the warm embrace of a mother whose love knew no bounds, a love that composed the most beautiful melody of their lives.

War of Nerves - A Collateral Damage

Meanwhile, Coast Guard shipbuilding project at ABC Shipyard had become a battleground for two senior officers, each vying for the coveted top technical position. Their rivalry had reached toxic levels, casting a dark shadow over the entire project and, unfortunately, pulling it into the murky waters of favouritism. While one of the officers was more deserving and was responsible for handling the project acquisition while other was with poor professional reputation, adverse rating and an ongoing court case against the service.

The project of Oil Spill Response Vessel was crucial for the Coast Guard, involving the construction of a new vessel that would enhance the capabilities of the maritime force. However, the clash between the contending officers had created an environment of distrust and chaos, leading to the accusation on decision to award the shipbuilding contract to a private shipyard under questionable circumstances.

As news of the controversy broke through leak by one of the coast guard officers, the media seized the opportunity to sensationalize the situation. Headlines screamed of favouritism, corruption, and a compromised shipbuilding project that put the nation's maritime security at risk. The shipyard involved, ABC Shipyard, found itself caught in the crossfire of a battle it had never signed up for.

Enter Vishal, a design officer who had once been a part of the Coast Guard team and was now working with ABC Shipyard. Alongside him was one of the shipyard's directors, determined to salvage the shipyard's reputation and set the record straight. Armed with facts, figures, and a commitment to transparency, Vishal and the shipyard director embarked on a mission to clarify the truth surrounding the controversial shipbuilding project. They issued press notes with replies to accusation, addressing the media's questions and concerns head-on.

Vishal, having been intimately involved in the project during his Coast Guard days, meticulously explained the technical aspects, the stringent evaluation process, and the impartiality that should have governed the decision-making. He emphasized that the shipyard had won the contract based on merit and capability, not favouritism. The shipyard's director echoed Vishal's sentiments, emphasizing the shipyard's commitment to delivering high-quality vessels for the defence forces. He reiterated that the decision-making process had been transparent and in compliance with all regulations.

However, the TV media, more interested in sensationalism than truth, persisted in framing the narrative to generate higher viewership. They focused on the rivalry between the senior officers, emphasizing the drama rather than the substance of the shipbuilding project. The negative coverage continued to tarnish ABC Shipyard's image.

Undeterred, Vishal and the shipyard's director doubled down on their efforts. They engaged with investigative journalists, providing them with comprehensive details of the project's evaluation process and the fairness involved in awarding the contract. Slowly, some print media began to publish more balanced articles, shedding light on the complexities of the situation. While Vishal and his Director sat in the waiting room of TV studio, media house clandestinely shoot the discussion while journalist was being explained with passion how media is wrong in presenting the story. However, only video part was flashed across, without presenting shipyard's voice response and explanation, just for the sensationalism.

In the end, the truth prevailed, even though as per government policy, contract award was preceded thorough scrutiny process by a Technical Oversight Committee consisting of independent and eminent technocrats specially appointed by the Ministry of Defence. The committee had cleared entire process of any abnormality. Another inquiry committee set up in Coast Guard to investigate the allegations also cleared all accusations, but the damage had been done. The sensationalism propagated by the TV media had left a lasting impact on ABC Shipyard's reputation. Despite the shipyard's efforts to clarify the situation and provide a clear picture, the public perception remained tainted.

The incident served as a cautionary tale, highlighting the power of media in shaping public opinion and the challenges faced by organizations trying to counteract sensationalism with facts. Vishal, while proud to have defended the shipyard's integrity, couldn't help but rue the unfortunate reality that sometimes, the truth becomes a casualty in the battle for headlines.

Building of Defence ship- Plethora of Challenges

The difficulties for Vishal began early stages of project when securing ship owner's approval for some of the equipment and machinery proved to be a prolonged ordeal and that slowed down the entire construction timeline. Vishal, however, remained undeterred. He knew that the success of the project depended on his ability to navigate through these challenges. With a tenacious spirit, Vishal personally engaged with the ship owners, addressing their concerns, and providing detailed explanations for the chosen equipment. He worked tirelessly to expedite the approval process, understanding that each day lost in bureaucracy was a setback to the project's overall timeline.

Simultaneously, another challenge emerged in the form of delays in getting design drawings approved by the Coast Guard. Rather than succumb to frustration, Vishal took a proactive approach. He initiated regular communication channels with Coast Guard officials, addressing their concerns promptly and incorporating necessary revisions in the design. He organized frequent meetings to provide updates on the progress and sought feedback to ensure alignment with their expectations.

The delays, though testing Vishal's patience, became an opportunity for him to showcase his skills. He fostered a culture of resilience within his team, motivating them to maintain focus and commitment despite the setbacks. Vishal's ability to keep everyone motivated and engaged became a crucial factor in maintaining momentum during challenging times.

As the project continued, Vishal's perseverance began to pay off. With the intervention of a new Coast Guard Overseer at shipyard and new project officer at Coast Guard Headquarter, things began to move faster now. Approval process became well-coordinated among all concerned, and project was now looking up. The shipyard, which had faced uncertainty and obstacles, now hummed with renewed energy and purpose.

Symphony of Skill: Construction of the Oil Spill Response Vessel

In the shipyard, where the scent of ocean breeze intermingled with the echoes of clanging steel, a dedicated team of technical heads toiled relentlessly to bring to life the Coast Guard's Oil Spill Response Vessel, the first in this type and class to be inducted into Coast Guard. Ship was propelled with Diesel-Electric propulsion and with options either in combination of diesel electric or only diesel or only electric as required. Main mission of the ship was to contain and recover the accidental oil spill at sea or near coast, in addition to normal patrol duty and external firefighting capability. It had the capacity to contain the oil spills, collect spilled oil water mix into ship's tank, process and then discharge recovered oil to the shore for disposal.

Each responsible for a specific vertical—steel hull, mechanical, piping, electrical and electronics, and many more—they all worked in unison, their collective effort guided by the orchestrating baton of Vishal, the Project Head.

At the steel hull section, the technical head meticulously oversaw the construction of the vessel's robust exterior. Steel blocks were carefully welded and shaped, forming the foundation of a vessel designed to brave the toughest maritime challenges. The rhythmic hammering and welding sounds reverberated through the shipyard as the hull began to take shape, a testament to the craftsmanship of the dedicated team.

Months passed, and the ship's hull took final shape. The sleek hull emerged from the skeleton of steel, and the intricate network of pipes and wires crisscrossed within the vessel's belly. Vishal's and teams' commitment to quality and precision reflected in every weld, every joint, and every component of the ship.

Down the line, the piping team worked tirelessly to create a network of pipelines that would carry essential fluids throughout the vessel. The interplay of pipes and valves resembled a complex circulatory system, ensuring the vessel's vital fluids flowed precisely where needed. The technical head of piping ensured that the intricate network adhered to the highest standards of safety and efficiency. Another professional, an ex-naval commander Salil Gupta had joined the OSRV team at site to assist Patra.

In the electrical department, wires and cables became the vessel's neutral network. Cable routing was an intense process and involved multi cable transit gland system for the first time on any defence vessel, while passing through watertight bulkheads. The technical head of electrical systems oversaw the installation of generators, switchboards, distribution panels, intricate control panels, control, and communication systems. Their meticulous work ensured that the vessel would be equipped with cutting-edge technology to navigate and operate effectively during oil spill Response operations.

The Guns were supplied by Coast Guard for its installation by shipyard. The gun mounting fitment was highly precision work and needed meticulous machining work on mating faces. The installation check was conducted by gun manufacturer and cleared which were tested by Coast Guard later after takeover of vessel.

Amidst this symphony of construction, Vishal, stationed in the shipyard's head office, took on the role of the conductor. His days were filled with coordination meetings, where he liaised with each technical head, ensuring a harmonious flow of information. The technical heads diligently provided updates on the project's progress, flagging any issues or bottlenecks that needed immediate attention. Budget control and monitoring meeting with higher management and finance team was regularly held to enable release of fund flow.

Vishal's coordination extended beyond the shipyard's gates. He liaised with equipment manufacturers, tirelessly chasing down technical data needed for integration. Meetings with Coast Guard authorities became a routine, as he sought timely approvals to keep the project on track. The project's success hinged on Vishal's ability to synchronize the efforts of each technical head and ensure a seamless flow of information between the shipyard and external stakeholders. It was crucial for Vishal to ensure that production plan as per chart along with all interconnected activities were adhered.

Having gone through and overcome the multiple challenges in past, first posed by flooding in shipyard and its after effect, allegation of favours in the media, and delay in design and equipment approvals, fruits of the efforts were slowly being realised.

Finally, the day arrived when the vessel was ready for launch. The ship, "Samudra Sevak," stood proudly at the synchro lift dock, a testament to Project teams' dedication and expertise. With much fanfare, ceremony and protocol involved, first Oil Spill Response Vessel was launched in 2008. The work was still half done, and post launching was the time to start energising installed equipment and machineries one by one to bring these alive.

Simultaneously, the mechanical and electrical system's technical head orchestrated the installation of the vessel's intricate machinery. Engines roared to life as the mechanical systems and auxiliary machineries were meticulously calibrated and tested. From propulsion to Pumps, AC and Ventilation, Refrigeration, RO Plants, Sewage Treatment, Power Generation, Electronics including Navigation and Communication, Deck machineries, Environmental equipment, Aviation systems, and every other component was scrutinized to ensure seamless functionality in the unforgiving marine environment.

As the Oil Spill Response Vessel neared completion, the collective efforts of the technical heads and Vishal materialized into a maritime marvel. The vessel stood as a testament to the dedication, skill, and coordination of a team united in their pursuit of maritime excellence. Together, they had orchestrated the construction of a vessel that would serve not just as a symbol of technological prowess but as a guardian of the seas, ready to respond to environmental challenges with precision and expertise.

As the ship started to come to finish line, heart of the ship an IPMS system, integrating all major equipment and machineries for centralised control and monitoring needed to be completed before ship can proceed for sea trials.

Ship's Stabilisation - Slow Manoeuvring

OSRV, due to its inherent role of oil spill response, was required to operate on slow speed during spilled oil recovery operation. The aft end area of ship was the main operational zone for oil response equipment and systems. The propulsion through main mode of ship's propellers was not a preferred choice and a special provision through the forward swing down type azimuth thrusters from Ulstein, Norway was considered. This provided necessary slow speed cruising with thruster in lowered position and doubled as side thruster when housed in to assist side way manoeuvring, and during dynamic positioning (DP) operation.

Naval ships are generally installed with active fin stabilizers which are more effective on higher speed, and are mechanical devices mounted on ship's hull side. They consist of fins those can swing angularly that extend outward from the hull into the water. These fins are controlled by hydraulic or electric actuators that adjust their angle in response to the ship's motion. By changing the angle of the fins, the stabilizers generate hydrodynamic forces that counteract the rolling motion of the ship. Active fin stabilizers are highly effective in reducing rolling motion across a wide range of sea conditions and ship speeds. They provide more precise control over the ship's stability and are often preferred for larger vessels and those operating in rough seas.

Passive Tank Stabilization System, on the other hand operates using the principle of fluid dynamics. It consists of a U-shaped tank located in middle of ship, along the sides and bottom of the ship's hull. These tanks are partially filled with water, and as the ship rolls, the water will tend to move toward rolling side with gravity, thus generating multiplying moment and further adds to the rolling. To mitigate this, in the passive tank stabilisation system, the gravitational force of water is reversed through a controlled mechanism by generating pressurised air asserting counter pressure to push back the water in opposite direction. The roll angle sensor and momentum are part of integral system. The water moves in opposite direction to the rolling side and thus creates a counter acting force that dampens the rolling motion.

Passive tank stabilization systems are effective in reducing the rolling motion of a ship, particularly at lower speeds and in moderate sea conditions. So OSRV was included with this provision as a first-time installation on any naval or coast guard ship. Its effectiveness was tested in sea trials with success.

Harmony of Seas: Symphony of Project Management

Vishal, at the helm of Oil Spill Response Vessel project, faced another challenging yet exciting endeavour. One of the most critical components of this state-of-the-art vessel was its complete automation through Integrated Platform Management System (IPMS), responsible for the seamless integration and control of various ship systems. Vishal knew that orchestrating this complex symphony of technology required a meticulous approach and effective coordination.

The IPMS, a technological marvel, was being supplied by a specialized global firm known for their expertise in naval systems integration. Vishal, aware of the importance of a harmonious collaboration, had already initiated a series of meetings and discussions with the IPMS supplier with the commencement of ship production. Understanding the intricacies of the system, Vishal worked closely with the system suppliers and Coast Guard to define the technical specifications and integration requirements tailored to the unique needs of the Oil Spill Response Ship.

Fortunately, another Coast Guard officer Commandant Shekhar, under whom Vishal has worked earlier, joined the parent organisation of IPMS manufacturer, after quitting Coast Guard and was on helm of affair on behalf of company. This was blessing in disguise and bode well for the project with better understanding and coordination. The parent company of the IPMS supplier's firm, a large global company manufacturing much equipment for the marine industry worldwide, was also responsible for supply of major machinery and systems for the project. Thus, Shekhar acted as nodal point for Vishal to interact with different factories of group company for better coordination.

However, the IPMS was just one instrument in the orchestra. Vishal needed to ensure that the data from other equipment and machinery suppliers were in perfect harmony with the IPMS timeline for integration. The challenge lay in coordinating with multiple suppliers, each providing critical technical inputs for their respective components, ranging from propulsion systems, major machineries, electrical equipment, oil spill Response equipment and other environmental monitoring equipment.

To streamline this process, a nodal hub was established in shipyard's design office for all stake holders. Regular meetings were held with representatives from each equipment supplier, creating an open channel for dialogue and information exchange. Vishal emphasized the importance of adherence to timelines and the necessity of providing comprehensive technical data to facilitate smooth integration. To ensure accuracy and completeness, Vishal worked closely with Coast Guard Overseer and each supplier to establish a standardized format for technical data submission. This not only expedited the integration process but also ensured that any potential discrepancies or conflicts were identified and addressed proactively.

The success of this coordination effort was evident as the project progressed. The IPMS supplier, armed with detailed technical data from various equipment and machinery suppliers, seamlessly integrated these inputs into their system design. The meticulous planning, effective communication and ABC shipyard's design teams' effort had transformed what could have been a cacophony of technical challenges into a symphony of synchronized systems.

As the Oil Spill Response Ship neared completion, Vishal reflected on the journey. The successful coordination between the IPMS supplier and manufacturer of Propulsion, Thrusters, DP system, Power Generation, Fire Control, Pumps, Tank Content Gauging and many other equipment was a testament to the power of effective project management and collaboration. The vessel, equipped with cutting-edge IPMS technology seamlessly integrated under watchful eye of shipyard's team, and coast guard overseer stood ready to be commissioned as a beacon of efficiency on the high seas.

Safety of Life at Sea and Distress Communication: IMO Regulations

The OSRV constructed under DNV Class rule were required to comply as mandated under International Maritime Organization (IMO) Regulation. The Global Maritime Distress Signal System (GMDSS) as such is a crucial safety protocol under IMO for all seagoing vessels governing its installation, testing, and maintenance aboard ships. GMDSS's key components such as Emergency Position Indicating Radio Beacons (EPIRBs), Search and Rescue Transponders (SARTs), MF/HF Radio Sets, Very High-Frequency (VHF) Radio, Inmarsat Satellite Communication Systems and Navtex Receivers. These features were thus formed part of vessel and were tested and certified for the ship.

> INMARSAT is a Satellite operated system that includes ship earth station terminals – Inmarsat B, C and Fleet 77. It provides telex, telephone and data transfer services between ship-to-ship, ship to shore, and shore to ship along with a priority telex and telephone service connected to shore rescue centres.
>
> NAVTEX is an internationally adopted automated system which is used to distribute MSI-maritime safety information, and includes weather forecasts and warnings, navigational warnings, search and rescue notices and other similar safety information.
>
> EPIRB is equipment to help determine the position of survivors during a Safety and Rescue operation. It is a secondary means of distress alerting.
>
> SART is primarily the Search and Rescue Radar Transponder. This is used to home Search and Rescue units to the position of distress which transmits upon interrogation.
>
> VHF Digital Selective Calling (DSC) is for calling between ship to ship, ship to shore or vice versa for safety and distress information mainly on high or medium frequency and VHF maritime radio.

The other mandatory systems under IMO conventions for Safety of Life at Sea (SOLAS) included and certified such as:

International Code for Application of Fire Test Procedures (FTP Code),

International Code for Fire Safety Systems (FSS Code)

International Life-Saving Appliances (LSA Code)

The Aviation Story- Flying Deck Operation

The OSRV vessel is designed to house Chetak helicopter inside its hanger and built with deck capability to land up to a naval Sea Kings helicopter on its flight deck in addition to Advance Light Helicopter (ALH). Features essential for helicopter operation including for night flying with essential visual aids are implemented on the ships. Fuelling system, Starting Rectifiers, Battery Charging, Helicopter Workshops were fitted in compliance to naval rules as well as international aviation rule CAP 437.

Vishal instrumented provisions from multiple sources after technical clearances from coast guard while Mr Patra ensured that his team installed these to perfection:

For stowage of helicopter, an indigenously built telescopic hanger with traverse guide was manufactured by shipyard and installed.

It had special helicopter fuel (AVCAT) tanks of stainless steel and an approved type fuelling system. The fuelling system was sourced from Norway and integrated.

Ship deck was fitted with a L&T circular landing grid, a stainless-steel thick plate with equidistance honeycomb holes all over the plate to facilitate harpoon arresting of helicopter once closer to deck.

Night helicopter operations on the deck of a ship involved a carefully set of procedures to ensure the safety of both the aircraft and the ship's crew. The ship's deck was fitted with deck perimeter lights all around along with other essential lightings.

The helicopter approach to the ship was by using predetermined flight paths and altitude profiles. For visual aid to approaching pilot, there was Glide Path Indicator and Horizontal Roll Bar fitted on hanger top, all supplied by Indian firms.

There was special communication equipment as per naval requirements for communication with control room or other aircraft which included Aero VHF, VHF/UHF, Identifying Friend & Foe (IFF)

A dedicated flight control Room was aft of wheelhouse with all the necessary control instrumentation on a control console.

A Scaled Model of OSRV

During Construction Phase

Engine Room of Ship

Main Switch Board Room

At Launching of Ship

Post Launching

During Trial Phase- IPMS Station

Wheelhouse of Ship

During Sea Trial Phase

Officers Mess- Ward Room

During Sea trials- Manoeuvring Trials

Final Test- Inclining Experiment

Inclining Experiment of ship is a crucial step before ship can proceed to sea for the trials. This experiment for OSRV was conducted at the finishing stage of construction, on a calm day to obviate heavy wind and wave effect. This was done to verify its stability characteristics and determine its final light ship weight and the position of the ship's centre of gravity.

The team of experienced naval architects from shipyard and designer Rolls Royce Marine, shipyard engineers, and DNV surveyors gathered to conduct the experiment on the day of experiment. The coast guard overseeing team at site witnessed the inclining experiment to verify the parameters. Vishal and Patra ensured beforehand that it goes as planned and all check boxes are ticked prior to the start of the experiment. There were several reasons why this was important.

In the experiment set of weights, about 15 tons each, four positioned on each side at earmarked distances, are moved across and back, and the angle of heel recorded at every stage. Process is repeated for other side once again. All the known missing weight for yet to be fitted equipment at the time of experiment are compensated. The fluid position in the tanks was recorded. These readings are then used in combination with hydrostatic data of ship for exploration of required parameters.

The primary purpose of the inclining experiment was to verify the stability characteristics of the ship. By determining the metacentric height (GM) and final light ship weight, shipbuilders had to ensure that the vessel meets regulatory stability requirements and is safe to operate in various sea conditions.

During the construction process, the weight of the ship changes slightly due to the addition or removal of equipment, machinery, and outfitting. Conducting the inclining experiment at the finishing stage allows shipbuilders to accurately determine the ship's final light ship weight, which is essential for stability calculations and safe operation.

Maritime regulatory bodies require ships to undergo an inclining experiment before they are certified for sea trials and operational use. By conducting the inclining experiment at the finishing stage, shipbuilders can ensure that the vessel complies with all applicable regulations and standards.

If the inclining experiment reveals any discrepancies or stability issues, shipbuilders could adjust or corrections before the ship proceeds to sea trials. This involves redistributing weight, modifying ballast arrangements, or making other changes to improve the ship's stability characteristics.

Ultimately, the inclining experiment verifies the ship's stability and weight distribution, shipbuilders can provide assurance that the vessel is seaworthy and can withstand the forces and motions encountered at sea without compromising safety. Once the inclining experiment was completed for OSRV and its report approved by DNV classification, ship came a step closer to completion.

Sailing to Success: Sea Trials of Oil Spill Response Vessel

As the construction of the Oil Spill Response Vessel reached its final stages, Vishal, the Project Head, along with team of all vertical heads led by Patra and Commander (Retd.) Salil Gupta, embarked on a next chapter in the shipbuilding journey—sea trials. The shipyard had been a hive of activity, with the local Coast Guard overseeing team and the nominated Coast Guard ship's crew joining forces with the shipyard's personnel for the crucial phase of testing and validation.

The team set their sights on Goa port, a coastal paradise that would serve as the proving ground for the vessel's capabilities. As they coordinated the logistics, Vishal worked tirelessly to ensure that the machinery & systems, yard material, ration, and crew needed for the sea trials were mobilized efficiently. Commissioning Engineers of machinery and equipment supplier also joined the endeavour, ready to validate the performance of their respective components.

Oil Spill Response Vessels was a sophisticated marvel, equipped with cutting-edge technology designed to tackle environmental disasters at sea. The sea trials of first of the three vessel were exhaustive, with a protocol that demanded meticulous testing of each system and component to ensure they met the contractual requirements and specifications.

The Coast Guard overseeing team worked closely with shipyard's team, reviewing the trial procedures, and ensuring that every aspect of the vessel's functionality was scrutinized. The ship's commissioning crew, responsible for taking over the ship once it passed the trials, familiarized themselves with the vessel's layout and systems.

As the vessel set sail for its maiden sea trial, the air was thick with anticipation and excitement. The sea trials comprised a series of manoeuvres and tests, ranging from speed, endurance, crash stop, dynamic positioning, various modes of propulsion, unmanned machinery mode, anti-roll tanks, assessments to emergency drills, Fire Control, Oils Spill Response Systems and many more. Trials of oil spill control systems were particularly daunting and of extra concern. Representatives from each system supplier closely monitored their equipment's performance, ready to address any issues that might arise.

The logistics of coordinating eight sea sorties, extending over two months for an exhaustive trial protocol, were staggering. Vishal and his team worked in seamless harmony, ensuring that each sortie was meticulously planned and executed. The crew aboard the vessel operated tirelessly, demonstrating the vessel's capabilities in various conditions and scenarios. The regular interaction and coordination between Vishal and the Coast Guard Overseer DIG Shailendra ensured that sea trials go smoothly as planned. Ship's Commanding Officer designate DIG Parkar was consulted prior planning of every sea sortie for the trials.

As the vessels got ready for test and trials, Ship's CO instructed his officers for ensuring stringent physical checks. It demanded not only meeting standards on paper but proving the vessel's capabilities through extensive testing and trials. He was ably supported by his engineering officer Commandant Vinod Panwar, Electrical Officer Commandant Manish Pandey and others. Compliance with approved specifications and adherence to the test trial protocol were non-negotiable. Every detail, from the hull's integrity to the functionality of the machinery and oil spill Response systems, was scrutinized to meet the highest standards.

Vessel underwent rigorous exercises, simulating real-world scenarios to demonstrate its effectiveness in oil spill Response operations. The oil spill Response equipment like Disc Skimmers, Weir Skimmers and Brush Skimmers, Aerial Spray System, Oil Booms for spill containment, Oil Discharge Monitoring Equipment, Oil Recovery & Discharge Systems were all tried and tested in actual scenario.

The ships commissioning crew was a bunch among the best in the Coast Guard and took enormous pain and efforts to not only learn all aspects of ship operation but ensured that every system takeover was not compromised and tested repeatedly before signing take over. The shipyard production team, under Patra's meticulous guidance, worked in harmony with the Coast Guard overseers. Continuous communication and collaboration were key as engineers and other technicians came together to complete the technologically advanced vessels.

At every sortie for sea trials, Vishal stood in wheelhouse to oversee and ensure smooth coordination among three parties to the trials i.e.

Shipyard, CG Overseer, and the Ship's Crew. Licensed crew consisting of Master Mariner, Chief Engineer and others crew essential to operate the vessel on shipyard's behalf were arranged for every sea sortie in advance, who would man the ship for the period of trials. Patra as production head along with Commander Gupta would plan and undertake the test and trial activities for each day. Coast Guard Overseer DIG Shailendra and his team oversaw entire technical verification, and ship's designated Commanding officer DIG Parkar and his team of other senior officers would monitor every trial activity. They would not only verify parameters as per trial protocol but make themselves familiarise with the ship's operation, as they would be operating it post-delivery of ship.

During the sea trials, wheelhouse was always crowded with Crew, Coast Guard teams, Service engineers and shipyard representatives. Wheelhouse was the hub of electronic instruments and display screens to monitor ship's operation. Some are engrossed on Electronic Chart and Display (ECDIS) for navigational route, while others monitored Navigational Radars, Echo Sounders, Speed log and other instrumentation. Communication team along with service engineers checked for Global Maritime Distress Singal System (GMDSS) and the MF/ HF sets. Master Mariner along with ship's designated Commanding officer and navigating officer were engaged on the propulsion control system assisted by few junior officers to oversee manoeuvring of the ship.

Technical in charges remained glued to IPMS control and monitor in the wheelhouse where touch screen provided running status and parameter for any system as desired. Be it Main Engines, Different Propulsion modes, Thrusters, Diesel Generators and electrical loads, Pumps, Fire Fighting system, Damage Control, Doors open close status, CCTVs, Tank's Content Gauging, and other important systems, all integrated and available for centralised monitoring and in some cases with limited control. Other team member associated with trials parallelly monitored systems through main IPMS screen in switch board room, machinery control room, and oil spill monitoring compartment.

With each successful sea sortie, the confidence in the Oil Spill Response Vessel grew. The meticulous planning, coordination, and dedication of the entire team paid off as the vessel met and exceeded the contractual requirements and specifications. Finally Dynamic Positioning system trials proved that all propulsive equipment and machineries are in perfect synchronization with each other and working in harmony. The Coast Guard overseeing team, impressed by the vessel's performance, gave their approval, marking a significant milestone in the project.

As the OSRV returned to the Goa port after the final sea trial sortie, Vishal looked back on the journey with a sense of pride and accomplishment. The collaborative efforts of the project team, the Coast Guard overseeing team, and the ship's crew had resulted in the successful validation of the vessel's capabilities. The first of the three vessels was now ready to join the Coast Guard fleet, a testament to the power of teamwork and determination in sailing towards success. Project team was now even more enthusiastic in completing other two ships of same class and went on with the production activities.

Now time had come for handing over of documentation, spares and other inventory items to Coast Guard ship and other agencies. While the delivery of design drawings, and manuals was completed by shipyard's design office, Vishal pushed DNV team for certificates for each equipment, machinery, and system inspected or tested by them. Final Class Certificate from DNV with vessel required notations, was the most important delivery document without which ship would not sail. Slowly spare parts and loose inventory was handed over to the ship staff. At the same time, a protocol for the agreed deficiencies for supply and defects was prepared and documented under pending liability, to be attended after the delivery of vessel.

In Sep 2010, once all aspects of ships delivery as per acceptance protocol neared finish, a formal handing over of vessel by Shipyard to the coast guard was held with laid down protocol and a gala dinner later. The function was attended by many coast guard dignitaries in Goa. The Dy Director General (Material & Maintenance) Inspector General Sushil Garg too joined in from Coast Guard Headquarters signifying importance of the project for the service. Once the news of handing over of first OSRV to Coast was conveyed to shipyard's Managing Director, a sigh of relief and jubilation was evident for the achievement.

As Oil Spill Response Vessel passed with flying colours and finally delivered, Vishal, Patra, Shankaran, Commander Gupta joined by other shipyard personal and the Coast Guard Overseer DIG Shailendra Kumar and his team stood proudly on the jetty, watching as the white colour, blue striped sleek silhouette, piloted by Coast Guard crew for the first time independently, disappeared into the horizon for its commissioning ceremony by Coast Guard at Mumbai Dockyard. Ship was commissioned by the Chief Minister of Mahasrastra amid the full ceremonial function and in presence of many other high dignitaries. Post ceremony, ship was visited by the invitees and their families. It received tremendous appreciation from the naval community and other regard to the rich quality of finish and spacious comfort in the accommodation and machinery compartments.

It was a story of teamwork, resilience, and unwavering determination—a testament to the power of collaboration in achieving greatness. It was also the time now to concentrate on balance two under production ships. As an appreciation, the management promoted both Vishal and Patra to next level Associate Vice President in recognition of their efforts post-delivery of vessel. Others responsible for the achievement were equally rewarded.

The Second Oil Spill Response Vessel

Review Meeting: Grilling Sessions by Government

A regular ritual in building of defence vessel was presenting the project progress and utilisation report of annual allocated capital budget during the quarterly progress review meetings. These meetings were no ordinary gatherings; they were convened at the Ministry of Defence and chaired by none other than the Joint Secretary (Acquisition Manager) for naval division where other members representative such as Additional Financial Advisor (Defence Finance), Technical Manager (Maritime), representatives from the Coast Guard Headquarters and the Coast Guard overseer at site. These meetings held paramount importance in ensuring the seamless progress of ongoing projects and take stock of allocated capital expenditure for the financial year.

Director (Technical) and Vishal sometimes along with Shankaran, head of Yard operations, and Commander Gupta representing ABC

Shipyard, approached these meetings with meticulous preparation, armed with detailed reports, comprehensive updates, and a clear vision for the future of each under-construction Coast Guard ship. As they entered the south block building from gate number 10 every time, to proceed to the conference halls of the Ministry of Defence, they carried not only the weight of their shipyard's reputation but also the responsibility of delivering vessels that would serve the nation with excellence.

The meetings were a confluence of minds, with Coast Guard authorities, acquisition managers, and shipyard representatives engaging in detailed discussions. Vishal, with his keen project management insights, and Mr Kamra, Director (Technical) with his deep knowledge and experience, presented the shipyard's progress, highlighted achievements, and addressed concerns or challenges.

The atmosphere in the meeting room was mostly serious as soon as Joint Secretary (Acquisition Manager) took charge. Director (Technical) and Vishal knew that the success of the project hinged on effective communication, transparency, and problem-solving during these crucial sessions. They faced tough questions, navigated intricate technical discussions, and provided clear explanations for any deviations or modifications made during the construction process. Their ability to convey the shipyard's perspective, articulate complex technical details, and address concerns with utmost professionalism earned them the respect and confidence of the Coast Guard authorities and the acquisition manager.

One of the recurring challenges discussed during these meetings was the issue of delays. Shipyard was transparent about the hurdles faced, attributing some delays to the prolonged approval process for drawings and the time-consuming task of selecting appropriate equipment. The meticulous scrutiny required for compliance often resulted in a lag that impacted the overall timeline of the project.

However, one of the most critical challenges arose from unforeseen circumstances. The force majeure clauses in the contract, including instance of severe flooding in the city and the shipyard, had triggered delays beyond the shipyard's control. ABC Shipyard were forthright in presenting these challenges to the Coast Guard authorities and the overseeing team. They explained how flooding in city had affected the shipyard's entire operations, including the destruction of stored equipment those awaiting installation. The force majeure events had created a domino effect on the project timeline, requiring careful consideration and, in some cases, the condoning of delays through formal processes. At last, an extension was approved by MoD for the delivery timeline extension but not to the extent shipyard had hoped for.

During these discussions, ABC Shipyard showcased their expertise in navigating complex contractual clauses and their commitment to finding equitable solutions. Their presentations were not just about highlighting challenges but also proposing mitigation strategies and amendments to the contract that would protect the interests of all parties involved. Through constructive dialogue and an unwavering commitment to transparency, ABC Shipyard ensured that the progress review meetings served as a platform for collaborative problem-solving. The Coast Guard authorities, recognizing the shipyard's commitment and proactive approach, worked along with Director (Technical) and Vishal to find common ground and ensure the project's success despite the unforeseen challenges.

The Coast Guard authorities, known for their stringent standards and commitment to maritime security, scrutinized every detail. They sought assurance that the vessels would not only meet but exceed expectations. The acquisition manager, the Joint Secretary, played a pivotal role in ensuring alignment between the shipyard's goals and the overarching defence strategy. As the shipyard's representatives left the Ministry of Defence after each meeting, they did so with a sense of pride, knowing that their efforts were contributing to the strength and capability of the

Coast Guard—a partnership forged in the crucible of progress review meetings that would continue to shape the maritime landscape for years to come.

Naval Project - A Merger of Convenience

During 2007, once a thriving shipbuilding unit Varun Shipyard, nestled close to the ABC Shipyard, faced the unfortunate fate of financial instability. The small private entity had proudly secured orders to construct six water tankers for the Navy, showcasing its potential in contributing to the country's defence infrastructure. However, the harsh realities of the maritime industry hit Varun Shipyard hard, pushing it to the brink of closure.

The impending shutdown not only posed a threat to the livelihoods of the shipyard's employees but also left the Navy in a precarious position, with crucial water tanker orders hanging in the balance. As news of Varun Shipyard's financial troubles spread, concerns loomed over the potential delays and setbacks in naval projects.

However, in the face of adversity, a neighbouring entity, ABC Shipyard, recognized an opportunity to step in and salvage the situation. ABC Shipyard, known for its deft handling of defence orders, saw the strategic advantage of acquiring Varun Shipyard and merging the two entities. The move would not only save Varun Shipyard from closure but also strengthen ABC Shipyard's position in the maritime industry. After intense negotiations, an agreement was reached, and Varun Shipyard officially became a part of ABC Shipyard. The transition was smooth, with Vishal spearheading the integration of the two teams and ensuring a seamless continuation of ongoing projects. The water tanker orders for the Navy were not only safeguarded but also expedited, showcasing the renewed efficiency and capacity of the merged shipyard.

Vishal, by now, General Manager at ABC Shipyard, known for his adept management of Coast Guard ship projects, was assigned the additional responsibility of overseeing the construction and revival of Varun Shipyard. With a reputation for effective negotiation and a keen understanding of naval and defence projects, Vishal was the ideal candidate to navigate the complexities of this rescue mission. Armed with full support from Mr Shankaran, Vice President (Yard operation) and Mr DP Garg, (Finance Head), at ABC Shipyard, all operations at the Varun shipyard were revived slowly once again.

The successful acquisition not only saved jobs at Varun Shipyard but also positioned ABC Shipyard as a key player in defence shipbuilding. Shipyard's adept handling of the situation earned them accolades within the navy and maritime community. The fortified shipyard went on to secure additional defence contracts, solidifying its role in strengthening the nation's maritime capabilities. The story of Varun Shipyard's revival became a testament to resilience, strategic vision, and the unwavering commitment to national defence.

Lost Ship - Revival of the Project

Vishal, the General Manager, once again found himself at the forefront of a challenging yet crucial project—the construction of water tankers for the Indian Navy. The project, once stalled due to unforeseen circumstances, required deft manoeuvring to get it back on course. Understanding the urgency, Shankaran VP and an ex-Commander Udit Banerjee, DGM Production, orchestrated a series of strategic meetings with Vishal, representing higher management for overall coordination and contract management. In these sessions, they outlined the criticality of resolving the constraints swiftly to ensure the timely completion of the water tankers.

With a united front, team presented a comprehensive plan to management in consultation with Mr Mahesh Rao an erstwhile head of shipbuilding at Varun Shipyard, who agreed to be onboard in interest of the defence project. This plan addressed each constraint methodically, outlining a course of action to overcome the challenges at hand. The constraints were multifaceted. Limited material availability, shortage of critical equipment, incomplete design data, and machinery and yard material constraints in the shipyard posed significant hurdles. The pressure to deliver all six water tankers to strategic naval locations in Mumbai, Kochi, and Karwar further intensified the challenge.

With unwavering determination, Vishal embarked on a journey to revive the water tanker project. Recognizing the need for strategic collaboration, he sought the guidance and handholding from Commodore Pradeep, Warship Production Superintendent (WPS) at Mumbai. To start with, duo had few meetings at WPS office in Mumbai to strategize. Commodore Pradeep with his wealth of experience and dedication to naval ship construction, and Commander Manoj, project head for Navy, joined forces with General Manager Vishal from ABC shipyard to breathe life back into the project. They forged a partnership that transcended the traditional client-contractor relationship, with the WPS team de facto becoming an integral part of the shipyard's team.

The first challenge was to align the project with the stringent standards of the Navy and ensure compliance with design specifications. Vishal orchestrated a harmonious collaboration between ABC Shipyard, the Navy's production team, the ship designer L&T Design, and the classification society, the Indian Register of Shipping (IRS). Together, they engaged in a meticulous process of design drawing approvals, ensuring that every aspect met the rigorous standards set forth by the Navy in the contract. Vishal's leadership and diplomatic skills played a pivotal role in navigating through the complexities of design modifications and enhancements.

Material management took enormous efforts to find the deficiencies and taking stock of equipment availability and balance to order. Finding record of procurement, sources of supply and revival of already installed equipment all was ultimately accomplished by a dedicated team set up for the purpose. Mr Mahesh Rao's input was extremely valuable to collate everything and contacting sources. This was also true for coordination of the drawings which was already approved or pending with IRS.

Throughout the project, site inspections were conducted to guarantee that the construction adhered to the approved design. Commodore Pradeep's hands-on involvement provided valuable insights, and the shipyard's team worked tirelessly under the direction of Deputy General Manager Banerjee, in charge of Production. As the collaboration flourished, the synergy between the shipyard, the Navy, and other stakeholders became increasingly evident. Vishal's adept management skills ensured seamless coordination, fostering an environment of trust and open communication. Vishal was ably assisted in project at head office by Dy Manager Anjan Chand, a junior shipwright, who last worked with WPS (Mumbai). With each milestone achieved, the water tanker project gained momentum. The once-struck project now sailed smoothly towards completion, a testament to the synergy forged through Vishal's leadership, Commodore Pradeep's guidance, and the collaborative efforts of all involved.

When the water tankers were finally unveiled, they stood as a symbol of resilience and cooperation. Vishal, Commodore Pradeep, and the entire team celebrated the successful revival of the project, recognizing that their collective efforts had not only fulfilled a crucial naval requirement but had also strengthened the bonds between the shipyard and the Indian Navy. At periodic interval, two each of these water tankers were delivered at Mumbai, Kochi and Karwar under ceremonial function.

In the end, the story of the water tanker project became a testament to the power of collaboration, effective leadership, and a shared commitment to excellence in naval shipbuilding.

An Unusual Reunion- Across the Meeting Table

It was a crisp morning at the Shipyard, in the conference room, a significant event was unfolding – A important meeting was underway on completion to finalise formal acceptance of a newly constructed first water tanker for the Navy. Ship named "Jal Sagar" had just completed her sea trails successfully and was being readied for delivery. Commodore Pradeep, WPS along with Commander Manoj were representing Navy's Overseeing team. Rajat, now a Commander in the Navy, was deputed for streamlining formal take over the vessel for Commodore of the Dockyard, Mumbai on behalf of the Admiral Superintendent, all sat on one side of the table.

Meanwhile, on the other side of the table sat Shankaran, Sr VP (Yard Operations), Vishal, AVP (Projects), Banerjee GM (Production), representing the ABC Shipyard an erstwhile Varun Shipyard, responsible for constructing the water tanker. They were accompanied by the team of their deputies from the shipyard. As the two sides of the event converged, destiny orchestrated a reunion between Rajat and Vishal, who had been batch mates from their Navy days beginning training. Three decades had passed since their initial journey together in the Navy. In those years, both had pursued their respective careers with dedication and determination. Vishal transitioned from the Navy to the private sector, while Rajat continued to rise through the ranks of commander within the naval service.

As the meeting unfolded, Rajat Singh found himself seated across from Vishal – a familiar face from his past, now in an unexpected role reversal. The two men, once comrades in the Navy, were now on opposite sides of the table – one representing the Navy, the other the shipyard. Their eyes met, and a faint smile tugged at the corners of Vishal's lips as he recognized Rajat. Despite the years that had passed, the bond forged during their navy training remained intact.

"Rajat, it's been too long," Vishal said, extending his hand across the table.

"Indeed, Vishal. It's good to see you," Rajat replied, shaking his hand warmly.

Once they exchanged greetings and informed how they are buddies from past from trainee days, Commodore Pradeep lightened the atmosphere with a joke.

Commodore Pradeep then proceeded to address the meeting and highlighted about balance work to be completed prior formal handing over at Mumbai, Naval Dockyard which is about a week later. He commended the efforts put in by shipyard in reviving the project, once envisaged as dead. A full road map was drawn for delivery of first vessel and for next five vessels still on berths for construction.

As Rajat rose to address the meeting, he couldn't help but notice the sense of pride emanating from Vishal. Memories from their naval training days flooded back – the camaraderie, the shared dreams, and the rigorous journey that had shaped their careers. In his speech, Rajat acknowledged the shipyard's commendable efforts in completing a vessel that met the Navy's exacting standards and spoke of the significance of the water tanker in supporting naval operations and how it would play a crucial role in maintaining the fleet's operational capabilities.

Shankaran, in turn, expressed his gratitude for the opportunity to contribute to the Navy's mission on behalf of shipyard. He highlighted the shipyard's commitment to excellence and how the project had become a labour of love for everyone involved.

As the meeting concluded and proceeded for formal lunch, Rajat and Vishal found a moment to catch up amidst the gathering. They reminisced about their early days in the Navy, sharing stories of the challenges they faced and the paths they chose. The unexpected reunion became a celebration of their individual successes and the shared pride in contributing to the nation's maritime capabilities. Vishal was relieved, knowing confidence and mutual respect developed for each other would make the task of delivery much easier.

The role reversal brought a sense of fulfilment to both men, realizing that their separate journeys had converged once again in the service of a common goal – the defence and prosperity of their nation. As they parted ways, Rajat and Vishal carried with them the memories of their intertwined destinies, grateful for the twists and turns that had brought them together on that momentous day at the Naval Dockyard.

Delivery of Ship -Worth Celebrating

The sun gleamed brightly over the calm waters as the newly constructed Water Tanker for the Navy stood proudly at the pier of Naval Dockyard, Mumbai. Shankaran, Vishal and Banerjee, the dynamic project heads, had navigated the complexities of ship construction with precision, and today marked the grand delivery of the vessel.

Just a day earlier, after hectic day long meeting amid noting down of pending liabilities, a formal acceptance document and certificates were signed and exchanged by both the parties signifying official takeover of vessel and paving a way for the ceremonial acceptance. A mandatory Class certificate issued by Indian Register of Shipping signifying technical compliances to marine regulations and readiness for sea operations was handed over too along with documents.

As naval dignitaries and esteemed guests gathered on the pier, the air buzzed with anticipation. The Water Tanker, meant to supply Fresh and Feed water to the ships and submarines at sea, a symbol of maritime prowess, awaited its ceremonial handover. Shankaran and Vishal, dressed in crisp suits, stood on the deck of the ship, ready to present it to the Navy with pride. The ceremonial function began with the playing of the national anthem, and the flag was hoisted on the Water Tanker. The shipyard's managers, supervisor, and workers, who had poured their sweat and expertise into the project stood alongside, their faces beaming with satisfaction as they witnessed the culmination of their hard work.

Admiral Superintendent of Naval Dockyard accompanied by Commodore Gagandeep, Commodore of Yards (COY), Commander Rajat, and other officers, staff and crew representing the Navy, were there to receive the ship. Shankaran and Vishal, flanked by their teams, symbolic handed over of the Water Tanker to Commodore Gagandeep, signifying the ceremonial transfer of ownership.

Amid the applause and cheers, on behalf of shipyard, Shankaran addressed the gathering, expressing gratitude for the collaborative effort that had brought the project to fruition. He acknowledged the dedication of the shipyard workers, engineers, and naval architects who had worked tirelessly to ensure the vessel's success.

Vishal echoed Shankaran's sentiments, emphasizing the importance of the Water Tanker in enhancing the Navy's capabilities. He spoke passionately about the innovative technologies incorporated into the vessel, showcasing the shipyard's commitment to excellence. Pleasantries were handed over to the invited senior officers from Navy on behalf of shipyard.

After the official handover, the atmosphere shifted to one of celebration. A gala lunch had been arranged, with a panoramic view of the Water Tanker as a backdrop. The pier transformed into a festive space, adorned with navy blue and white decorations. High-ranking naval dignitaries, shipyard executives, and other invitees mingled, exchanging stories and insights. The shipyard workers, now in casual attire, joined the festivities, proud to see their creation become a focal point of admiration.

The lunch was a symphony of flavours, with a diverse menu that catered to every palate. Conversations flowed freely as guests savoured the food, sharing anecdotes and laughter beneath the azure sky.

As the day drew to a close, the first Water Tanker "Jal Sagar" stood as a testament to the successful collaboration between the shipyard and the Navy. Shankaran and Vishal, with a sense of accomplishment, watched as the vessel prepared to embark on its maiden voyage, ready to serve the nation's maritime needs. Commodore Pradeep, Warship Overseer and commander Manoj, the project officer for Navy, both had a sigh of relief writ on their faces as only they knew how a project almost considered dead once by Navy, was revived under his watch and now ready to serve the Navy.

The ceremony and gala lunch marked not only the delivery of a Water Tanker but also the forging of enduring bonds between the shipyard, the Navy, and all those who had played a role in bringing this maritime marvel to life.

Once the euphoria of delivery celebration was over, the entire production team along with navy's overseeing team, once again got immersed in the nitty gritty of completing remaining five water tankers, to be delivered two each at Mumbai, Karwar and Kochi.

Navigating the Storm: Battle Against Financial Turmoil

In the aftermath of the global financial collapse of 2008, ABC Shipyard, once a beacon in the maritime construction industry, found itself navigating treacherous waters. The shipbuilding sector, battered by the economic downturn, witnessed a sharp decline in new orders, and existing contracts faced the spectre of cancellation. As international shipyards across the globe struggled to stay afloat, ABC Shipyard was not exempt from the financial tempest. As the global recession unfolded, major shipping companies worldwide were grappling with financial uncertainties, causing a significant slowdown in the demand for new vessels. ABC Shipyard, like many others, faced a sudden and unprecedented downturn in business. Orders that once flowed steadily into the shipyard now dwindled, and the harsh reality of cancelled contracts loomed overhead.

To compound the situation, the shipyard had taken on significant loans to fund ongoing projects and expansions. The sudden and severe contraction of the shipbuilding market meant that ABC Shipyard was unable to generate the revenue needed to service these loans. As a result, it teetered on the brink of defaulting on its loans, sending shockwaves through the industry. The financial strain not only impacted ABC Shipyard's ability to meet its financial commitments but also raised questions about the management of funds within the private shipyard. Faced with this dire situation, the shipyard's leadership took swift and decisive action. They engaged in transparent communication with financial institutions, seeking restructuring of loans and relief measures to weather the storm.

To exacerbate the situation, whispers of financial mismanagement and fund diversion began to circulate. Concerns about the shipyard's financial health and potential irregularities prompted stakeholders to scrutinize ABC Shipyard's books more closely. In response, an insolvency process was initiated, and a forensic audit was conducted to delve into the financial intricacies.

The forensic audit conducted through an expert by consortium of banks stated to have uncovered a web of financial mismanagement, revealing instances of fund diversion and questionable financial practices within ABC Shipyard. The shipyard's leadership was under scrutiny for their role in these irregularities, further eroding the trust of investors, clients, and financial institutions.

As news of the forensic audit's findings spread, the shipyard's reputation crumbled, and speculation about its imminent closure gained momentum. The shipyard's leadership, facing both financial ruin and a tarnished image, found themselves in a dire predicament. The company was subjected to further scrutiny by income tax and the revenue intelligence authorities which are still under ongoing investigations.

The insolvency process, a mechanism designed to salvage what could be salvaged from the wreckage, led to ABC Shipyard's descent into its closure in 2019. With debts piling up, assets diminishing, and a tainted reputation, the shipyard struggled to find a lifeline that could pull it from the depths of insolvency.

As shipyard fought to regain stability, the new management control put in by banker's consortium, implemented stringent cost-cutting measures, including workforce reductions and operational streamlining. The shipyard's dedicated employees, understanding the gravity of the situation, rallied together to support their workplace and protect their livelihoods. They were somehow able to complete and deliver those vessels which are almost complete only under the financial control of bankers and could recover some of the debt from delivery.

The Coast Guard's and Naval project under Vishal's hand were delivered to their respective owners in a big sigh of relief. Unfortunately, one of the Navy's another signed projects under construction at another unit of shipyard suffered the consequences of closure along with many other commercial ship projects for different owners.

The closure of ABC Shipyard marked the end of an era, a poignant reminder of the devastating impact the 2008 financial collapse had on industries worldwide. It also served as a cautionary tale about the importance of transparent financial practices, ethical leadership, and the need for resilience in the face of economic adversity.

The shipyard employees were left in lurch as any hope of getting their long pending salary and statutory dues was dwindling day by day. Same was the case with suppliers, awaiting their payment dues. As the shipyard finally went into closure, and under NCLT proceedings, employee could do nothing but only prayed for a miracle. With the spectre of closure looming over ABC Shipyard, Vishal found himself at a crossroads. With his livelihood threatened and the maritime industry in turmoil, he knew he needed to chart a new course for his career. Determined to stay afloat amidst the uncertainty, Vishal began exploring alternative avenues, casting his net far and wide in search of opportunities.

The shipyard's closure sent shockwaves through the maritime construction sector, prompting a revaluation of financial practices and a renewed commitment to transparency within the industry. As the waves of change washed over the shipbuilding landscape, the lessons learned from ABC Shipyard's tragic voyage would shape the industry's future, ensuring that its compass was set toward more stable and ethical waters.

Closure not only brought about end of a vibrant shipyard's function, but it also brought end to many bright careers and monetary losses to small contractors and suppliers. At the end ultimate loss was not monetary but "loss of immense knowledge and expertise in shipbuilding gained over the period by its engineers".

PART 7

EASTERN COAST CALLING

Setting Sail Again: Quest for Professional Fulfilments

The closure of ABC Shipyard cast a shadow over the shipbuilding industry. Vishal, embarked on a quest for new opportunities, seeking uncharted waters where his skills could continue to flourish. Word of Vishal's expertise and skills had reached the ears through a fellow mariner who had earlier moved to an upcoming shipyard on the east coast in Kolkata. Recognizing Vishal's potential through referral, a distant company, into heavy engineering and fabrication for railways wagons, that had recently diversified, and had embarked into shipbuilding, called him up for an interview.

On the specific day of interview, Vishal reached Kolkata office of East Coast Shipyard Ltd. He was driven from airport to the corporate office and met company Vice President Aniket, a smart young and enthusiast man belonging to promotor's family, who was heading the shipbuilding division. Vishal was ushered into the chairman's chamber by Aniket for a formal interview. After about one hour of discussion on various aspects of shipbuilding and considering Vishal's experience in managing defence project, he was taken in then and there, and asked to join as soon as possible as its Vice President, Projects & Marketing.

Upon arrival to Kolkata from Mumbai, Vishal found himself facing the Ganges River, a stark contrast to the familiar shores of his previous endeavours. He was greeted with a warm welcome by his new colleagues and managers. He quickly settled into his role, immersing himself in the new endeavour. The new chapter in Vishal's career unfolded against the backdrop of Navy projects, each one presenting its own set of challenges and opportunities. His leadership and project management skills, honed over years at ABC Shipyard, proved valuable as he navigated the intricacies of naval construction. The satisfaction of contributing to the defence capabilities of the nation added a sense of purpose to his work.

Vishal was now directly assisting Aniket at corporate office in handling of ongoing naval and other projects and for the marketing, who was also guided by retired Commodore Deshmukh working as Senior Vice President. His next cabin occupant at corporate office was a retired Major General Bhattacharya who was handling army's Balley Bridge project for the company. Both occasionally apprised him about deeper functioning of the company.

In addition to naval project, Vishal was also assigned a key role in the construction of a Coastal Research Vessel, a scientific vessel for the government. This opportunity allowed him to diversify his experience, delving into the complexities of a vessel that would play a pivotal role in advancing scientific exploration. He knew his experience of Oil Spill Response Vessel with coast guard would be of immense help here. With his wealth of experience and expertise, he soon became an invaluable asset to the team, earning the respect and admiration of his peers.

The Life in City of Joy - Kolkata

In the summer of 2017, Payal found herself uprooted from the bustling streets of Mumbai and transplanted into the vibrant city of Kolkata. Her husband, Vishal, had found an opportunity to work at a prestigious organisation in the city, and they had relocated in pursuit of this new chapter in their lives. But for Payal, the transition was anything but smooth.

While their elder daughter Monisha was already married and settled in Gurgaon, the younger daughter Reena worked in Mumbai and lived independently closer to workplace at Cuffe Parade, and that made Payal move to Kolkata with Vishal much easier.

Accustomed to the fast-paced lifestyle of Mumbai, Payal initially found the slower pace of Kolkata disconcerting. She missed the familiar faces of her friends and the comforting chaos of her old neighbourhood. Their new home, an upscale condominium called Urbana at EM Bypass in Kolkata housing many prominent personalities of Kolkata, felt imposing and unfamiliar. As the days passed, Payal struggled to find her footing in this new environment. She felt isolated and out of place amidst the sea of unfamiliar faces. But all of that was about to change with the arrival of Durga Puja, the grand festival celebrated with unparalleled fervour in Kolkata.

As the city came alive with the sounds of drums and the scent of incense, Payal found herself swept up in the whirlwind of activity that surrounded the festival. The condominium complex was transformed into a hive of excitement and friendship, as residents came together to celebrate the joyous occasion.

From participating in cultural performances to decorating the premises with elaborate pandals, there was a flood of action and interaction among the community. Payal found herself drawn into the festivities, eagerly participating in the preparations, and revelling in the sense of belonging that permeated the air.

In the midst of the celebrations and a month-long preparation, Payal forged bonds with her fellow residents that would last a lifetime. She discovered a sense of community and belonging that she had sorely missed since leaving Mumbai. As the days turned into weeks and the weeks into months, Payal and Vishal's social circle in Kolkata continued to grow, bringing them immense satisfaction and joy. This social circle extended to the Army, where Vishal and Payal had forged bond with few senior army officers and their families they came across and would often meet over weekends.

No longer did Payal feel like a stranger in a strange land. Kolkata had welcomed her with open arms, and she had embraced it wholeheartedly. From that moment on, there was no looking back for Payal. She had found her place amidst the hustle and bustle of the city, and she wouldn't have it any other way.

The Challenges of Work

As days turned into weeks and weeks into months, Vishal found himself thriving in his new environment, relishing the opportunity to contribute to meaningful projects that would have a lasting impact. The bustling port city of Kolkata provided the perfect backdrop for his professional growth, offering a vibrant tapestry of culture and commerce that fuelled his passion for the maritime industry.

From marketing to bidding for the new tenders was additional challenge and Vishal got well versed soon. With each passing day, Vishal's confidence grew, and he found himself embracing the challenges and opportunities that came his way with gusto. The closure of ABC Shipyard, once a daunting obstacle in his path, now seemed like a distant memory as he forged ahead on his journey, charting a new course toward a brighter and more prosperous future in the maritime world.

The challenges were abundant, but Vishal's resilience and adaptability shone through. The change of scenery, the new faces, and the different shipyard dynamics rejuvenated his passion for maritime engineering. The shipyard in Kolkata became a canvas for Vishal to paint his expertise, and he thrived in an environment that embraced innovation and excellence. As the scientific research vessel took shape, he reflected on the journey that had brought him from the brink of closure at ABC Shipyard to the forefront of naval and scientific endeavours in Kolkata. The transition had not only saved his career but had opened doors to opportunities he had not envisioned.

Vishal's tale became one of resilience, adaptation, and the ability to find new horizons even when faced with the stormy seas of industry challenges. The shipyard in Kolkata, with its naval projects and scientific aspirations, not only provided him with a new professional home but also affirmed that, in the world of maritime engineering, every career has the potential to set sail on a course filled with exploration, growth, and uncharted success.

Waves of Reflection: Journey to Rediscovery

Two years had already passed by since Vishal had embarked on a new chapter in Kolkata. First of the navy's Fuel Tanker and Research Vessel each were successfully delivered. The vibrant city and the promise of exciting projects had initially fuelled his enthusiasm, but as time unfolded, a sense of disillusionment crept in slowly. Despite the picturesque surroundings and the cultural richness of Kolkata, Vishal found himself yearning for the dynamic challenges and fast-paced life he had left behind.

In the confined quarters of the shipyard, Vishal felt the slow pulse of life in the city permeate his professional journey. The projects lacked the dynamism and complexity that had once fuelled his passion at ABC Shipyard. Since the shipyard was new, the methods adopted were at times unconventional in nature. The decision-making power and autonomy he had relished in his previous roles were notably absent, leaving him yearning for a more stimulating and fulfilling professional experience. Canvas for demonstrating his potential was restricting and narrowing day by day. The organisation was primarily attuned with railways manufacturing and on many occasions, Vishal found his failing in convincing the top management about traditional difference in shipbuilding processes, which sometime are time consuming and not comparable to other sector. This posed more challenges and difficulties to sustain in such environments.

As the days turned into months and then into years, Vishal's dejection grew. The satisfaction derived from his work waned. The city, while enchanting, couldn't compensate for the professional challenges he craved. It became clear to Vishal that his journey in Kolkata had run its course, and it was time to weigh anchor once again. At personal front he had very cordial relations with the top management, but the situation was not turning into his favour.

One afternoon, as the day was coming to an end, Vishal made a pivotal decision. He would call it a day at the East Coast Shipyard, seeking new shores and fresh challenges. It wasn't an easy decision; the bonds forged with colleagues and the memories created in the city added emotional weight to his choice. The decision, however, was a testament to Vishal's unwavering commitment to professional fulfilment. He understood that true satisfaction came not just from the familiarity of a place but from the alignment of one's passions and ambitions with the challenges presented.

As he resigned and bid farewell to his colleagues in Kolkata, Vishal's heart brimmed with a mix of nostalgia and anticipation. The next port of call remained uncertain, but the allure of new challenges and a revitalized sense of purpose guided his course.

Vishal set sail once again, ready to navigate the unpredictable currents of the maritime industry in pursuit of a career that would both challenge and inspire him. The lessons learned in Kolkata became a valuable part of his journey, reminding him that professional satisfaction was not just about the destination but the exhilarating voyage towards it.

The move once again was difficult for Payal, who by now was totally engrossed in newfound social network in Kolkata and started to love the life there. The pain they felt in the eyes of their friend circle was not something they had wished for. But eventually this painful return was not they could avoid. They received a warm send off from everyone and left with promise to remain connected in life.

PART 8

AN ENTREPRENEUR CALL

An Entrepreneur Journey

Vishal, by now an accomplished naval engineer, after not a very fulfilling tenure at shipyard in Kolkata, found himself at a crossroads. The corporate environment, laden with limitations, had left him yearning for a more dynamic and fulfilling professional journey. Rather than succumbing to disillusionment, Vishal saw this juncture as an opportunity for a new beginning.

He first dabbled with question where should he head now? Back to the Mumbai city he has made his home for more than a decade, or back to the Delhi where he has spent his childhood and extended family lived. Monisha, his elder daughter who was married by and now lived in Gurgaon, ultimately clinched the decision to move from Kolkata to Gurgaon.

With a wealth of experience and a burning entrepreneurial spirit, Vishal decided to forge his own path. He envisioned a consultancy firm that would bring his expertise directly to the forefront, unencumbered by the constraints of traditional corporate structures. The prospect of steering his destiny and contributing to projects on his terms fuelled his determination.

Armed with a clear vision and a wealth of industry knowledge, Vishal set up his consultancy firm. The company, named "Marine Dynamics Solutions LLP," aimed to provide innovative, client-centric solutions for a range of maritime challenges. Vishal's reputation in the industry ensured that the venture garnered immediate attention and respect. Despite the covid pandemic setback, the firm slowly gained momentum, securing work for technical solutions.

As the firm started traction, Vishal found himself not only at the helm of a venture but also at the forefront of innovation into other industries. Vishal's decision to venture into entrepreneurship had not only rekindled his professional satisfaction but had also positioned him securely in the technical domain. Looking back at his journey, Vishal realized that sometimes, dissatisfaction with the status quo could be the catalyst for transformative change. By seizing the opportunity to create something new, he had not only rejuvenated his own career.

As Vishal delved into the intricate world of marine consultancy, he recognized the need for innovative solutions, particularly in the realm of defence and security. It was during this period that he crossed paths with Vivex Technologies Ltd, a Gurgaon based company specializing in defence sector manufacturing with a focus on secure communication networks and surveillance systems. Seeing the potential for collaboration, leadership at Vivex Technologies and Vishal decided to join forces. Together, they aimed to work in ventures that could revolutionize the coastal security establishments by offering cutting-edge solutions tailored to their specific needs.

This opened new horizons for both companies. Vishal's marine consultancy brought a deep understanding of maritime operational requirements, while Vivex Technologies contributed its expertise in advanced defence communication technologies, including secure surveillance solutions suited to marine environment. Their new venture embarked on a mission to identify and capitalize on potential business opportunities within the defence and security sectors. Vishal's knowledge of the maritime industry complemented Vivex Technologies' capabilities, creating a synergistic partnership that promised innovation and excellence.

Together, they began developing integrated solutions that addressed the evolving challenges faced by marine security establishments. From enhancing communication system on naval establishments to implementing state-of-the-art surveillance technologies for coastal and airport security, their collaborative efforts aimed to raise the bar for defence and security solutions.

Today, as Vishal looked back on his over 42 years in the maritime industry, he found fulfilment in knowing that his journey was far from over. The marine consultancy he has embarked is not just a business venture; it is a manifestation of his unwavering commitment to advancing the field he loved.

Life Ahead- A New Beginning

As Vishal nearing the end of his illustrious career, he finds himself standing at a crossroads, contemplating the vast expanse of the journey that still lay ahead. After years spent navigating the intricate workings of ships and shipyards, he, and his wife, Payal, are now ready to embark on a new adventure—one that would take them far beyond the confines of their professional lives and into the uncharted territories of nature, travel, and spirituality.

With their younger daughter Reena also married by now and both children along with their spouses are doing well in their careers and happy, they see partial retirement on the horizon. Vishal and Payal are beginning to dream of a life filled with exploration and discovery. They longed to immerse themselves in the breathtaking beauty of the natural world, to traverse rugged mountain trails and meandering rivers, to witness the awe-inspiring spectacle of sunrise over distant horizons and sunset on remote shores.

But their aspirations extended beyond mere travel. They are seeking to deepen their connection with the world around them, to delve into the mysteries of the universe and unlock the secrets of the soul. For Vishal and Payal, retirement is not simply an end to one chapter of their lives, but the beginning of a new and infinitely more profound journey—a journey of self-discovery, growth, and enlightenment.

As they slowly plan to bid farewell to the rigors of Vishal's professional career, Vishal and Payal have started setting their plans into motion. They intend trading the comforts of city life for the rugged simplicity of mountains, embarking on a simpler existence that would take them to the farthest reaches of the land. But amidst the breathtaking beauty of the natural world, Vishal and Payal also found time for introspection and reflection. Meditating beneath trees, practicing yoga, go on tracking and seeking out the wisdom of spiritual masters in remote mountains.

With each passing day, Vishal and Payal feel themselves drawing ever closer to the heart of existence, their souls nourished by the beauty and serenity that surrounded them. And as they journey deeper into the uncharted territories of nature, travel, and spirituality, they are discovering a profound sense of peace and fulfilment that transcended the boundaries of time and space.

For Vishal and Payal, contemplated retirement is not an end, but a beginning—a chance to embrace life in all its richness and diversity, to savour each moment as a precious gift, and to walk hand in hand into the boundless possibilities of the future. And as they stand together on the threshold of this new chapter, they know that their greatest adventure is yet to come.

ABOUT AUTHOR

$\mathcal{W}$ith over four decades of experience in the marine sector, I have traversed the diverse landscape of the Navy, Coast Guard, and the corporate world. Beginning my journey in the Indian Navy as Artificer, and honed skills as a naval engineer, navigated the intricacies of ship design, maintenance, and operations that gave me with valuable hands-on experience, laying the foundation for my future endeavours.

Later transitioning to Coast Guard as a Senior Design Officer that spearheaded critical shipbuilding projects and in turn gained wealth of knowledge and expertise. My understanding of naval architecture, marine systems and technology proved instrumental in the execution of some of the critical vessels for the coastal defence. With my subsequent venture into the realm of private shipyards, I continued to make significant contributions in execution of defence shipbuilding projects.

About Author

As a writer, I have tried to bring to life the rich tapestry of my experiences from naval training to full career in the marine sector, offering readers a rare glimpse into the inner workings of shipbuilding and the challenges and triumphs encountered along the way. In "Riding the Waves," I share my journey with readers, inviting them to embark on a voyage of discovery and enlightenment. From the hallowed halls of the Indian Navy to the bustling shipyard, this story is a testament to the passion, dedication, and unwavering determination in the pursuit of excellence in the marine sector.

www.ingramcontent.com/pod-product-compliance
Lightning Source LLC
LaVergne TN
LVHW041915070526
838199LV00051BA/2624